LINKING READING ASSESSMENT TO INSTRUCTION

AN APPLICATION WORKTEXT FOR ELEMENTARY CLASSROOM TEACHERS

LINKING READING ASSESSMENT TO INSTRUCTION

AN APPLICATION WORKTEXT FOR ELEMENTARY CLASSROOM TEACHERS

Arleen P. Shearer
Hillsborough County Public Schools
Tampa, Florida

Susan P. Homan
University of South Florida
Tampa, Florida

St. Martin's Press
New York

To our families for their continuing love and support.
Thank you,
Mary, Louis, Ruth, Murray, Richard, Todd, and Lauren.

Editor: Naomi Silverman
Managing editor: Patricia Mansfield-Phelan
Project editor: Amy Horowitz
Production manager: Patricia Ollague
Art director: Sheree L. Goodman
Text design and composition: Barbara Bert
Cover design: Sheree L. Goodman
Cover art: Steve Stankiewicz

Library of Congress Catalog Card Number: 92-50027

Manufactured in the United States of America.
8 7 6 5 4
f e d c b

For information, write:
St. Martin's Press, Inc.
175 Fifth Avenue
New York, NY 10010

ISBN: 0-312-04765-7

PREFACE

WHAT IS THIS BOOK ABOUT, AND WHY DID WE WRITE IT?

Linking Reading Assessment to Instruction—a worktext for individuals who are or intend to be teachers—reflects our cumulative efforts at preparing teachers for the classroom. Over the years we have been teaching reading methods, reading diagnosis, and corrective reading courses, we have found that many of the texts we use with our students provide excellent information on a theoretical level, but few offer adequate practice activities in instructional and assessment techniques appropriate for the elementary classroom. We decided to write this text to make these kinds of application activities widely available. It is intended as a supplement to be used along with the "standard" texts normally used in pre-service or in-service courses.

As students go through this book, they will experience the world of decision making in teaching and have many opportunities to engage in making decisions of their own. A major premise of this book is that *instructional decision making is critical to effective teaching practices*—and that classroom teachers must be knowledgeable in various types of formal and informal assessment techniques, appropriate methods for collecting data, and ways to accurately interpret that data in order to make sound decisions. We believe our worktext provides the opportunities needed to prepare teachers for the vitally important work of instructional decision making.

As we searched for ways to support and extend the theory and concepts presented in college-level reading methods and reading diagnosis textbooks, we often discussed with our students and colleagues the different activities we developed. We learned that the most effective activities are those that mirror most closely the realities of the elementary-level classroom.

This worktext is designed to share with you our application exercises that have proven to be most successful. All of the activities have been field tested in the college classroom, all of the assessment measures have been used with elementary-grade children, and most of the data used for interpretation are based on case studies.

We acknowledge that students who complete this worktext will not be experts in assessment and diagnosis. We do hope, however, that it will help them to become more aware of ways to learn about children, the appropriate use of formal and informal assessment techniques in the teaching process, and the steps to take in applying these techniques to instructional decision making.

OUR APPROACH TO THE READING PROCESS

The application activities in this book are grounded in the ideas and work of individuals who have made important contributions to theory and practice in reading instruction, including Clay, Downing, Harris, Betts, Powell, Searfoss, and Gillet and Temple. Although a complete development of reading theories is beyond the scope of this worktext, we strongly recommend that students use the suggested readings cited at the end of each chapter to build a strong conceptual base.

HOW THIS BOOK IS ORGANIZED

Chapter 1 provides detailed definitions of the terms *diagnosis* and *assessment* and explains the differences between them. This chapter also explains the range of variation from skills to strategies, provides information on integrating assessment and instruction, and presents various forms of record keeping.

In **Chapter 2** students engage in self-evaluations of their prior knowledge of reading concepts and theory. An Anticipation Guide, a Self-Assessment of Proficiency in Reading Diagnosis, and a Self-Scoring Cloze Pretest: Reading Instruction are provided for this purpose, along with suggested readings for review of specific information students may need based on their individual self-assessments.

Chapters 3–8 are the core of this worktext. Each chapter includes brief explanations of major reading and assessment concepts, followed by examples and guided- and independent-practice opportunities for gathering information, administering assessment techniques, analyzing and interpreting assessment data, and using this data for instructional decision making. Each chapter ends with a brief summary and a list of suggested readings. These chapters cover structured observations and the interview (Chapter 3), using standardized test scores (Chapter 4), identifying problem readers (Chapter 5), the Informal Reading Inventory (Chapter 6), evaluating comprehension strategies (Chapter 7), and assessment of word recognition knowledge and spelling stages (Chapter 8).

Chapter 9 covers grouping and instructional decision making; many of the activities in this chapter call on and provide for synthesis of knowledge and information gained throughout the text.

Three appendices at the end of the book enhance its usefulness for students and instructors: Directions for the Directed Listening-Thinking Activity (Appendix A); Directions for the Language Experience Approach (Appendix B); and copies of the Oral Reading Behavior Analysis Form, Summary Sheet, and the Cloze Test Applied Error Analysis Sheet (Appendix C).

In addition, an extensive **glossary** is provided. All glossary terms are highlighted in boldface the first time they appear in the text.

An **Instructor's Manual** provides information on how to use this worktext to supplement the most widely used reading methods, reading diagnosis, and assessment texts; effective teaching strategies; chapter summaries with suggested discussion questions; and additional activities.

ACKNOWLEDGMENTS

We would like to extend our thanks to our colleagues who reviewed the manuscript at its various stages. Along with the four anonymous reviewers, we would like to thank Arlene Barry, University of Kansas, Lawrence; Wendy Bishop, Florida State University; Bonnie Ericson, California State University, Northridge; Jane Hornberger, Brooklyn College; Jane S. McGraw, California State Polytechnic University, Pomona; and Mark Sadoski, Texas A&M University.

All successful books are the result of positive efforts from a team of people. We would like to thank all of the reviewers for their insights and suggestions. We appreciate the guidance and support of Naomi Silverman and Amy Horowitz of St. Martin's Press.

We wish to give special thanks to Stephanie Heaton, who typed our original manuscript. We also thank Kathleen Keller, who was the first editor to express interest and faith in our project.

During the editing process, our one and only hard copy and computer disk were destroyed in a fire. Along with all the staff at St. Martin's Press, our colleagues at the University of South Florida and Hillsborough County Public Schools were extremely supportive, patient, and helpful. Many thanks to all of you!

Arleen Shearer
Susan Homan

CONTENTS

9 GROUPING AND INSTRUCTIONAL DECISION MAKING   219

CHAPTER 1

ASSESSMENT AND DIAGNOSIS DEFINED

In this chapter, a framework is provided for **assessment** and **diagnosis**. Definitions of terms are given, as well as a method of planning classroom assessment and diagnosis.

ASSESSMENT VERSUS DIAGNOSIS

There can be confusion between the meanings of *assessment* and *diagnosis*, and, in fact, these terms are often used interchangeably. In this worktext, *assessment* is the broader term, defined as the systematic process of gathering information about students. Assessment is ongoing in all classrooms for all children throughout the school year. The results of assessment may identify students who need a more intensive examination of their strengths and abilities. This intensive examination is *diagnosis*.

The purpose of both assessment and diagnosis is to make instructional decisions about how best to help students. Results of assessment and diagnosis help the teacher determine which instructional objectives to teach (or reteach), what methods and strategies to use, and what materials are appropriate. If a teacher engages in assessment and diagnosis and does not use the results, then the measurement activity was unproductive. Just as assessment that does not result in a decision is a useless activity, decisions based on inadequate information may be unfounded.

Reading assessment is the gathering of information to determine a student's developmental reading progress; it answers the question "At what level is this student reading?" In addition, assessment procedures provide information about the student's **comprehension** and **decoding** strategies, interests, attitudes, and communication skills. Teachers are engaged in assessment when they observe student behavior, review **standardized tests**, administer teacher-made tests, and use questioning procedures. Assessment occurs most often informally and in the context of instruction.

If a student is not progressing as expected, then diagnosis is in order. A question posed in diagnosis is, "What are the student's strengths and abilities?" A teacher may also ask, "What does the student need to maximize his or her reading progress?" This type of questioning requires a more in-depth examination of the student's sight vocabulary, comprehension strategies, and word-analysis strategies and skills.

SKILLS VERSUS STRATEGIES

There are several views, or theories, of reading, one of which is the subskills, or **bottom-up model**. This model holds that readers acquire the ability to read by learning a hierarchy of skills in both word recognition and comprehension. In this model, instruction concentrates on the acquisition of separate subskills in decoding and comprehension, such as phonics, context clues, and main idea identification.

A more conceptually driven model of reading is the **top-down model**. In this model, the reader uses what he or she already knows about the reading topic to process the information. This model has created a new way of thinking about reading instruction: Reading is perceived as "sampling, selecting, predicting, comparing, and confirming" what the reader sees and expects to see (Harris & Hodges, 1981). A top-down model of instruction emphasizes the use of prior knowledge to develop hypotheses and make **predictions**.

Yet, an effective reader uses skills as well as appropriate strategies; as Vacca, Vacca, and Gove state, "Reading is rarely totally top-down or bottom-up" (1991, p. 21). The reader who comes across an unfamiliar word may apply a strategy to unlock the pronunciation and/or meaning. However, if the reader has a limited number of skills in word recognition, he or she may be hampered in applying a strategy. Students need to have available many options to assist them in successfully gaining meaning from text. Thus, to hold an "only skills" or "only strategies" view can be limiting in instruction and unfair to students. These two approaches can work in concert to provide maximum success in reading instructional practices. The meshing of these two approaches can be considered an "interactive model" of reading instruction (Vacca, Vacca, & Gove, 1991).

As with instruction, assessment and diagnosis should not focus on either skills or strategies. The evaluation of both are essential in the decision-making process.

Teachers who hold to a strict skills model of reading assess specific skills such as finding the main idea, sequencing, final *e* rule, or syllabication. This approach is common in many schools because of the use of criterion-referenced measures and basal mastery-skill tests.

Assessment that uses both models of reading would also examine the student's strategies in processing print and gaining meaning. The teacher may wish to evaluate **metacognitive skills**; **schema**, or background knowledge; **linguistic strategies** in word analysis, such as the use of **syntactic** and **semantic cues**; and knowledge of **text structures**. Whatever the teacher's model of reading, once the student's areas of strength and abilities are evaluated, those areas showing greatest need are prioritized and addressed through specific instruction.

In addition to studying the student, the teacher may investigate aspects of the classroom environment. Here the teacher asks, "What factors within the classroom need to be removed, lessened, or added to assist the student in the learning process?" The teacher investigates teacher-learner-task-strategy interaction and infers possible changes in materials, grouping procedures, and feedback and reinforcement techniques.

Thus, assessment is more than the administration of a test or battery of tests and, in fact, can utilize a variety of techniques that include "alternative" or "performance" measures. Diagnosis examines what the child can and cannot do, what skills and strategies are used, and what the child needs to improve reading performance. We concur with Harris and Sipay (1990), who state that the core of diagnosis is not gathering the information but, rather, interpreting the information so as to establish a plan to correct learning problems and/or enhance learning. By questioning and observing, the teacher comes closer to making the appropriate instructional decisions for every child.

In summary, the questions that guide assessment and diagnosis are the following:

At what reading level is the child functioning?

What are the child's reading interests?

What is the child's attitude toward reading and/or school?

What are the child's strengths and abilities?

What strategies and skills does the child need to foster his or her reading progress?

INTEGRATING ASSESSMENT AND INSTRUCTION

We need to view assessment not as a separate teaching act but as an integral part of teaching. Balancing the teaching of the regular curriculum and implementing ongoing assessment is, indeed, a challenging task. But assessment and diagnosis can be facilitated by scheduling time for the process and by being aware of the instructional activities that can be used as **informal tests** for assessment.

The major method of collecting classroom assessment data is teacher observation of student behavior. By this, we mean **systematic observation** during which the teacher records observational data by using **anecdotal records** or data-collection forms.

Observation can be greatly simplified if the teacher focuses on one or two students each day. If this plan were employed, a teacher could observe twenty to forty children in a month. In most instances, focused observations are sufficient for the majority of children who are adequately progressing in reading.

Instructional activities provide informal, yet real, opportunities for assessment. For example, children's knowledge of **story elements** can be evaluated by using **story grammar** and **story frames**. During large-group guided-reading instruction, the teacher can focus on one child's comprehension abilities by using questioning. In a group activity, the teacher can employ a data-collection form to record oral reading errors, and strengths and weaknesses in comprehension.

In addition to observing children, one of the best ways to gain information is to interview each child. While this can take up to 10 minutes per child, the information can be invaluable. Time needs to be scheduled for interviews. If the teacher schedules 30 minutes twice a week for interviews, it would be possible to confer with six students per week, or twenty-four children in one month.

When diagnosis is warranted, the teacher will require at least 30 minutes for individual testing. Because not all of the diagnostic information needs to be derived in one sitting, several meetings should be scheduled. Diagnosis may only need to occur twice a year with the child who needs more intensive assistance. The initial diagnosis provides information to plan appropriate instruction. The second diagnostic session provides additional planning information and records the child's progress, which may not be sensitively measured by standardized **norm-referenced tests**. Remember, throughout the year, informal observation and other assessment measures will monitor the child's progress.

RECORD KEEPING

As the teacher engages in assessment and diagnosis, the information needs to be kept in a file. Some observation records, writing samples, and instructional activities used in assessment and which document a child's progress can, and should, be shared with the child and included in the **portfolio**. However, test protocols and data collected for instructional decision making are more appropriately kept in a teacher file. Whatever method a teacher uses to record progress, assessment and diagnostic data should be kept in a place that facilitates teacher review.

SUMMARY

Even though assessment and diagnosis are often used interchangeably, the terms are delineated in this worktext. *Assessment* is considered to be the broader term, signifying the continuous gathering of information on students, while *diagnosis* refers to the in-depth examination of an individual student's strengths and needs. The purpose of both assessment and diagnosis is to help the teacher make instructional decisions. Teachers will not engage in diagnosis with all children; only those children who are not progressing as expected. Teachers should, however, conduct assessment every school day.

CHAPTER 2 / SELF-EVALUATION

The purpose of Chapter 2 is to examine your knowledge of and attitudes toward reading processes and methodology. Three instruments are provided for that purpose.

An *anticipation guide* is a type of **advanced organizer**. Its focus is on your opinions of reading diagnosis and corrective reading instruction. This instrument is mainly a springboard for discussion and a method of promoting thinking about reading diagnosis.

Next, a *self-assessment* instrument attempts to measure your comfort level regarding your own reading diagnosis expertise. After identifying the areas in which you feel less confident, you may want to concentrate on developing those knowledge areas. You may wish to retake this instrument when you've completed the course to determine your own growth.

Last, this chapter provides a *self-scoring* **cloze test** to measure your knowledge of reading philosophy, methodology, and processes. With this instrument, you could identify those areas that need review or further study. All three instruments are intended to be schema-activating devices.

ANTICIPATION GUIDE
READING DIFFICULTIES AND DIAGNOSIS

Directions: Using the key below, indicate your position on each numbered statement under the column headed "Prior to Learning." With a partner, discuss your conclusions and rationales. You do not have to agree with your partner, but make sure you can substantiate your responses. Be prepared to discuss each statement with the class.

When you have finished discussion and/or this course (as directed by your instructor), reevaluate each statement and indicate your position under the column headed "After the Learning."

Key:
SA = Strongly Agree
 A = Agree
 D = Disagree
SD = Strongly Disagree

Prior to Learning	After the Learning		
_____	_____	1.	Children who are competent language users can still experience severe reading problems.
_____	_____	2.	There is usually one identifiable cause of a reading difficulty.
_____	_____	3.	Poor teaching is a contributing cause of 50 to 60 percent of all reading problems.
_____	_____	4.	Standardized reading tests provide sufficient information to identify children who have reading problems.
_____	_____	5.	Diagnosis of reading problems should be conducted by a specialist in that field.
_____	_____	6.	Diagnosis means a one-on-one evaluation using a rigorous test or battery of tests to determine a cause and a remediation procedure.
_____	_____	7.	There is a specific instructional sequence to help a child improve his or her reading abilities.
_____	_____	8.	Instructional follow-up should focus on reading skills and should provide the child opportunities for guided and independent practice.
_____	_____	9.	Grouping students into no more than three reading groups is the most effective classroom management method.
_____	_____	10.	**Formal tests** provide the most reliable information to help the teacher make instructional decisions.

SELF-ASSESSMENT OF PROFICIENCY IN READING DIAGNOSIS

Directions: Rate your *level of proficiency* in performing each of the behaviors listed below by circling the number to the *right* that best describes you. If you do not know what the behavior is describing, circle the number to the *left* of the behavior. The value of this assessment lies in your honest appraisal of your abilities. Assessing your skills honestly will help you identify the areas in which you should concentrate during the course. Review this form again after you have finished this course to determine your level of progress.

Behaviors	Limited Skill		Some Skill		Strong Skill
1. Conduct systematic observations of students.	1	2	3	4	5
2. Interview children, parents, and/or teachers.	1	2	3	4	5
3. Administer and interpret the *Concepts about Print Test.*	1	2	3	4	5
4. Read and follow directions in test manuals.	1	2	3	4	5
5. Interpret standardized reading-test scores.	1	2	3	4	5
6. Administer a standardized reading test.	1	2	3	4	5
7. Develop questions on different levels of comprehension.	1	2	3	4	5
8. Informally assess a child's reading comprehension abilities.	1	2	3	4	5
9. Informally assess a child's word-analysis skills and strategies.	1	2	3	4	5
10. Administer an **informal reading inventory (IRI).**	1	2	3	4	5
11. Determine students' reading levels based on IRI results.	1	2	3	4	5
12. Record a student's oral reading **miscues.**	1	2	3	4	5
13. Analyze a student's oral reading miscues.	1	2	3	4	5
14. Develop a cloze test.	1	2	3	4	5
15. Interpret a cloze test.	1	2	3	4	5
16. Synthesize test data and form conclusions.	1	2	3	4	5
17. Write a summary diagnostic report.	1	2	3	4	5
18. Determine if a student is in need of corrective instruction.	1	2	3	4	5
19. Group students for instruction based on test data.	1	2	3	4	5
20. Assess a student's content reading abilities (science, math, social studies, etc.).	1	2	3	4	5

SELF-SCORING CLOZE PRETEST
READING INSTRUCTION

Directions: This is a modified cloze test with key words deleted. This exercise is designed to review some basic concepts about reading philosophy and reading methods. Complete the cloze by writing in each blank space one word that best completes the meaning of the sentence and passage.

Learning to read involves the mastery of a complex series of processes.

Instruction has been based on the belief that the _____ process is
1

composed of a set of acquired skills in _____ recognition and
2

comprehension. Word-recognition skills include _____ of letter-
3

_____ correspondences (phonics), _____ analysis,
4   5

_____ words, **context** _____ , and dictionary skills.
6   7

    Comprehension skills are frequently categorized as _____ ,
8

inferential, and critical skills such as finding the main _____ ,
9

determining fact from _____ , and predicting.
10

    The best reading instruction methods following the skills model provides

a balanced program of word _____ and comprehension
11

instruction. The method most commonly associated with the skills model has

been the _____ **reading method**.
12

    Currently, reading instruction has taken more of a comprehension focus

that promotes an **interactive** _____ of reading. In this theory, the
13

reader activates _____ knowledge as well as identifies the
14

important elements of _____ structure. The reader constructs
15

visual _____ of text information in order for the reading process to
16

be _____ . Reading in this model is not viewed as a separate skill in
17

the language _____ but, rather, as an integrated process with
18

listening, speaking, and _____ . Methods associated with the
19

integrated theory include the language ＿＿＿＿＿＿ approach,
20

＿＿＿＿＿＿ -based reading, and whole ＿＿＿＿＿＿ .
21   22

The child brings to the learning many factors that influence his or her

readiness for reading instruction. For example, the child's background

＿＿＿＿＿＿ relate to his or her ability to learn to ＿＿＿＿＿＿ . In
23   24

addition, the child's level of ＿＿＿＿＿＿ development has, perhaps, the
25

greatest impact on determining future ＿＿＿＿＿＿ in reading.
26

Traditional concepts of readiness have been expanded to include concepts

about ＿＿＿＿＿＿ . The awareness of print may be directly related to the
27

child's ＿＿＿＿＿＿ to begin formal reading instruction.
28

Knowledge of how reading develops as well as the various

＿＿＿＿＿＿ for teaching children to read is essential if the teacher is to
29

engage in assessment and ＿＿＿＿＿＿ decision making. The teacher's
30

philosophy of reading will influence not only the method(s) selected to teach

reading but also the methods of informal and formal diagnosis used in the

classroom.

Scoring: Check your answers with the key, and count the correct responses. If
you scored 18 or more correct, your knowledge is excellent. If you scored 12–
17 correct, your knowledge is adequate, but a brief review of reading methods
and philosophies is recommended. If you scored less than 12 correct, a more
intensive review is needed.

Answer Key

1. reading	11. recognition	21. literature
2. word	12. **basal**	22. language
3. knowledge	13. model	23. experiences
4. sound	14. prior	24. read
5. structural	15. text	25. language
6. sight	16. images	26. success
7. clues	17. meaningful	27. print
8. literal	18. arts	28. readiness
9. idea	19. writing	29. methods
10. opinion	20. experience	30. instructional

SUMMARY

You had opportunities to assess your levels of knowledge and awareness regarding reading theory, methods, and assessment. After you have completed this course, return to these exercises and check your progress.

SUGGESTED READINGS

Barr, R., & Johnson, B. (1991). *Teaching reading in elementary classrooms: Developing independent readings.* New York: Longman.

Cheek, E. H., Flippo, R., & Lindsey, J. (1989). *Reading for success in elementary schools.* Chicago: Holt, Rinehart & Winston.

Duffy, G., & Roehler, L. R. (1989). *Improving classroom reading instruction: A decision making approach* (2nd ed.). New York: Random House.

Mason, J. M., & Au, K. H. (1990). *Reading instruction for today* (2nd ed.). Glenview, IL: Scott, Foresman/Little, Brown.

Strickland, D. S., & Morrow, L. M. (Eds.). (1989). *Emerging literacy: Young children learn to read and write.* Newark, NJ: International Reading Association.

Vacca, J. L., Vacca, R. T., & Gove, M. K. (1991). *Reading and learning to read* (2nd ed.). New York: HarperCollins Publishers.

3 / STRUCTURED OBSERVATIONS AND THE INTERVIEW

As teachers instruct, they naturally observe their students to determine if they understand, if they respond appropriately, and if they like the activities. This is the essence of classroom assessment.

Observation means watching children engaged in learning and noting how they perform tasks and what they produce in those tasks. Observation occurs simultaneously with instruction and is the most commonly used form of assessment in the classroom. It is a powerful tool of classroom assessment (Farr & Carey, 1986).

Observation can provide the teacher with information regarding students' vision, hearing, speech, general health, and emotional and social needs. Teachers can gain insight into students' problem-solving strategies and can identify possible problems in reading and learning. Having a keen sense of observation and utilizing the technique in a structured manner can provide teachers a great deal of information for decision making.

This chapter provides a rationale and method for structured observation and a variety of observation checklists organized by developmental reading stages to assist in that process. To evaluate a child's emergent reading stage, a *Modified Concepts about Print Test* is also given. This informal test is a structured task that utilizes observation of students' responses to examine the development of print concepts. Last, the interview format is discussed as a means of gathering information on the reading strategies of students at the early and fluent literacy stages.

STRUCTURED OBSERVATION

In keeping with the concept of assessment as noted in Chapter 1, observation is one source of data, but not the only source, on which a teacher makes hypotheses. Observation data should be an additional piece of the puzzle, not the only piece. Used regularly, observation can help detect students' deficiencies early, so they can be corrected and reading failure avoided.

Most often, teachers engage in informal, unstructured observation without writing formal notes or keeping a written record. This informal method of observation assumes the teacher's memory is consistently reliable; however, evidence suggests teachers are overconfident in their ability to remember events without keeping records (Richert, 1988). We highly recommend that all planned observations be recorded.

During structured, or systematic, observation, the teacher keeps a written record and usually has a specific purpose for conducting the observation. Information is documented and can, therefore, assist in instructional planning. If a portfolio is maintained on each child, the structured observation can provide developmental information gathered over time.

One method of systematically collecting information is to develop an anecdotal form that has each child's name and a space to note significant events. Clark, Clark, and Lovett (1990) propose such a form for mathematics assessment; here is a sample of that form for reading:

Student	Date	Comment	Action Required
Paul A.	10/15	Predicted story events	None
Cindy D.	10/15		
Ernie F.	10/20	Knew story elements	None
Tammy H.	10/20	Didn't sequence	Work with sequencing

A class list as above used on a weekly basis provides helpful information for future instruction. At the end of a week, the teacher can also see which students were not observed. While a roster-type format is easy to use, we know a teacher who makes observation notes on address labels and then peels them off and adheres the labels to the children's assessment files. Either approach, or one of your own invention, will effectively structure your observation activity.

Checklists are often helpful in gathering information because the teacher can complete the checklist quickly and efficiently. Both informal checklists (developed by the teacher) and commercially prepared checklists serve as screening devices to identify children with particular problems.

Judgment errors can be minimized by collecting information in a variety of observation settings, such as individual instruction, group instruction, daily reading assignments, and informal group discussions. In structured observation, the teacher should know what to look for and utilize a combination of methods for gathering data.

The accuracy and reliability of observation also depend on the individual carrying it out. The observer must be able to differentiate between facts observed and inferences drawn from those facts. For example, "Harvey is a poor reader" is an inference; "Harvey omits whole lines of print" is an observable fact. Only the observable behaviors of the child should be recorded. Inferences and interpretations come when a number of observations, together with other measures, are synthesized. Utilized in this way, observation can be a powerful assessment tool that provides information not gleaned by other methods.

STRUCTURED OBSERVATION OF THE EMERGENT LITERACY STAGE

During the past twenty years, changes have been occurring in the way we look at **reading readiness** or **prereading skills**. Thanks to the work of Clay (1991) and Downing (1979), we now view the first reading tasks as **cognitive processes**, not **perceptual processes**.

A child's understandings about print are vital to his or her success in early reading. When a child understands that print carries a message, he or she has developed the first and most important prereading concept. Other print concepts include **directionality** (left to right) and a knowledge of terms like *word, letter, top, bottom, front, back, first,* and *last.* In examining the child's understanding of these terms in relation to reading, the teacher should note whether the child is able to distinguish a word from a letter or the space between words, and to identify the front of the book and the top of the page.

Lack of knowledge of these concepts may result in **cognitive confusion**, which can inhibit reading progress. Marie Clay (1985) has developed the *Concepts about Print Test,* which assesses a child's concepts about print using one of two "prompts" (specially designed picture books), *Sands* or *Stones.* Included in this chapter is the Klesius and Searls (1985) adaptation of Clay's test, which covers six cognitive areas of prereading awareness but does not use a standard prompt. Rather, any picture book can be used in the administration of their test.

Using the Modified Concepts about Print Test*

To administer the Klesius-Searls test, the teacher would need one illustrated children's book and a pencil with an eraser. With these in hand, the teacher would follow the guidelines below, and record the child's responses on the answer sheet.

1. **Directional Terms:** *Front* **and** *Back*

   Hand the student a simple illustrated children's book with the spine facing the child, and say:

   > "Show me the front of the book."

   > "Show me the back of the book."

2. **Function of Print**

   Open the book to a place where the print is on one page and a picture is on the other (have marked for quick location). Then say:

   > "Show me which page tells the story."

   Observe whether the child points to picture or print. If the child points to the page of print, say:

   > "Show me where I begin to read on this page."

*Adapted from Marie Clay's *Concepts about Print Test* by Janell P. Klesius and Evelyn F. Searls (1985). Reprinted with permission.

3. **Left-to-Right Direction**

Stay on the same page, and say:

"Show me where I go next when I read." (Observe whether the child sweeps finger across the printed line from left to right.)

Then ask:

"Where do I go from there?" (Note whether the child correctly makes the return sweep to the left and drops down one line.)

4. **Concepts: *First* and *Last***

Turn to a new page, and say:

"Point to the first word on this page."

Then say:

"Point to the last word on this page."

Then ask:

"Where is the end of the story?"

5. **Directional Terms: *Top* and *Bottom***

Turn to another pair of pages with print on one and a picture on the other. Point to the printed page, and say:

"Show me the bottom of the page."

"Show me the top of the page."

Point to the picture, and say:

"Show me the top of the picture."

"Show me the bottom of the picture."

6. **Word and Letter Boundaries**

Hand the child the eraser end of a pencil, and say:

"Circle one word."

"Circle two words."

"Now circle one letter."

"Circle two letters."

TEST OF PRINT CONCEPTS
Answer Sheet

Student _____ Age ____ Grade ____ Date _____

Examiner _____

	Correct	Incorrect

1. **Directional Terms**

   Front _____ _____

   Back _____ _____

2. **Function of Print**

   Print function _____ _____

   Start at top left _____ _____

3. **Left-to-Right Direction**

   Left to right _____ _____

   Return to lower line _____ _____

4. **Concepts**

   First _____ _____

   Last _____ _____

   End of story _____ _____

5. **Directional Terms**

   Top (page) _____ _____

   Bottom (page) _____ _____

   Top (picture) _____ _____

   Bottom (picture) _____ _____

TEST OF PRINT CONCEPTS (CONTINUED)
Answer Sheet

	Correct	Incorrect
6. **Word and Letter Boundaries**		
1 Word	_____	_____
2 Words	_____	_____
1 Letter	_____	_____
2 Letters	_____	_____

Interpretation and Recommendations

_____

_____

_____

_____

_____

_____

_____

_____

_____

_____

_____

_____

_____

_____

SAMPLE
Test of Print Concepts
Answer Sheet

Student _Yolanda_   Age _8_ Grade _2_ Date _10/15/93_

Examiner _L. S._

	Correct	Incorrect
1. Directional Terms		
Front	✓	
Back	✓	
2. Function of Print		
Print function		✓
Start at top left	✓	
3. Left-to-Right Direction		
Left to right	✓	
Return to lower line	✓	
4. Concepts		
First	✓	
Last	✓	
End of story		✓
5. Directional Terms		
Top (page)	✓	
Bottom (page)	✓	
Top (picture)	✓	
Bottom (picture)	✓	

SAMPLE (CONTINUED)
Test of Print Concepts
Answer Sheet

	Correct	Incorrect
6. Word and Letter Boundaries		
1 Word		✓
2 Words		✓
1 Letter	✓	
2 Letters	✓	

Interpretation and Recommendations

Yolanda has developed most of the print concepts measured by this test. However, there are three areas that need further observation. When asked which page tells the story, Yolanda pointed to the picture. She was unable to identify a word or the end of the story. She needs direct instruction on the concept of *word* and continued exposure to print.

A C T I V I T Y

USING THE TEST OF PRINT CONCEPTS

The purpose of this activity is to practice interpreting the results of a test of print concepts.

Directions: Using the information given on this form, interpret the results and provide a recommendation for instruction.

Student _Derek_____ Age _6_ Grade _1_ Date _9/15/93_

Examiner _Smith_____

	Correct	Incorrect
1. Directional Terms		
Front	✓	
Back	✓	
2. Function of Print		
Print function	✓	
Start at top left		✓
3. Left-to-Right Direction		
Left to right		✓
Return to lower line		✓
4. Concepts		
First		✓
Last		✓
End of story		✓

USING THE TEST OF PRINT CONCEPTS (CONTINUED)

	Correct	Incorrect
5. Directional Terms		
Top (page)	✓	
Bottom (page)	✓	
Top (picture)	✓	
Bottom (picture)	✓	
6. Word and Letter Boundaries		
1 Word		✓
2 Words		✓
1 Letter	✓	
2 Letters	✓	

Interpretation and Recommendations

_____

_____

_____

_____

_____

_____

_____

_____

_____

_____

_____

Using the Observation Checklist: Emergent Literacy Stage

The purpose of the *Observation Checklist: Emergent Literacy Stage* is to provide a structured way to observe one child or a small group of children who are in a prereading, or **emergent literacy**, stage (readiness to primer basal reader levels). The form aids the teacher in examining a child's oral language, the **speech-to-print match**, letter and word recognition, **auditory perception**, and **visual motor skills**. An observation period may cover any one section or several sections of the form.

Preparing for the Observation

Before beginning the observation period, you will need several 3-by-5-inch cards and a storybook. If the class or group has developed a **language experience approach (LEA)** story chart previously, it, too, can be used for this observation. Prepare a name card for each child participating in the observed activity. On other cards, print four to eight words from the storybook or LEA story chart, being sure to include some nouns. You also need to select words that have the following characteristics:

1. one word that has several rhyming words
2. two pairs of words that have the same beginning sound
3. two pairs of words that have different beginning sounds
4. two pairs of words that have the same ending sound
5. two pairs of words that have different ending sounds

If you use a storybook for the observation period, you should follow a **directed listening-thinking activity (DLTA)** format. If you are unfamiliar with the DLTA or the LEA, you should familiarize yourself with these procedures. Directions for these activities are in the appendices.

Conducting the Observation

Use one observation form for each child being observed. Write the child's name in the upper left-hand corner and his or her grade level placement in the designated space. Follow the specific directions below for each section.

I. Oral Language Skills

Follow directions for LEA and DLTA. If using the LEA, item 7 on the checklist will not apply.

II. Speech-to-Print Match

1. Say: "Point to the words as you read them." Note whether the child shows a one-to-one correspondence with the word read orally and the word to which he or she pointed.

2a. Say: "Point to where you should begin reading." Note whether the child points to the first word in the story or first word on the page.

2b. (DLTA only) Say: "Where is the story?" Note whether the child indicates that the print, not a picture, provides the story.

3a.   Say: "Show me with your finger how to read the story." If the child stops at the end of the first line, ask: "Where do I go from there?" The child should indicate the left-to-right pattern with the left sweep to the next line.

3b.   (DLTA only) Say: "Show me the front of the book"; "Show me the end of the story."

4.   Using word cards already prepared, say: "Read these words from the story."

5.   Using name cards already prepared, place them in front of the children, and say: "Find your name on these cards."

III. Letter and Word Recognition

1.   Say: "Point to a lowercase letter in the story."

2.   Say: "Point to an uppercase (capital) letter in the story."

3.   Using the word cards, ask the child(ren) to match the cards to the words in the story.

4.   Select several of the noun word cards, and ask the child(ren) to draw a picture of each word.

IV. Auditory Discrimination Skills

1.   Say: "What word rhymes with _____?" (Use the word you selected from the story that has a number of possible rhymes.)

2.   Say: "Tell me whether these two words from the story start with the same sound." (Use the selected four pairs.)

3.   Say: "Tell me whether these two words from the story end with the same sound." (Use the selected four pairs.)

V. Visual Motor Skills

1.   Provide a stimulus set of letters on paper. Ask the children to trace the letters.

2.   Give each child his or her name card, and ask the children to write his or her name on a piece of paper or on the chalkboard.

Recording the Observation Data

Record the date of the first observation under the heading Obs. I (Observation I) and the second under Obs. II (Observation II). Using the key DA = Developing Adequately or NE = Needs More Experiences, evaluate the child's responses. If you believe the child is developing adequately in the area indicated on the form, place a check in the DA column. If you believe the child needs more work in the area, place a check in the NE column. Record additional comments on the back of the sheet.

For example, if the child was observed on two occasions, the top of the form would look like the following:

Student _Paula_   Grade _3_

Examiner _M. Watts_

	Obs. I Date 9/15/93		Obs. II Date 10/30/93	
	DA	**NE**	**DA**	**NE**
I. Oral Language Skills				
1. Participates freely in group discussions.	✓		✓	
2. Speaks in complete sentences.		✓		✓
3. Relates words and pictures.		✓		✓

OBSERVATION CHECKLIST
EMERGENT LITERACY STAGE

Student _____   Grade _____

Examiner _____

	Obs. I Date _____		Obs. II Date _____	
	DA*	NE*	DA*	NE*

I. Oral Language Skills

1. Participates freely in group discussions.   ____ ____ ____ ____

2. Speaks in complete sentences.   ____ ____ ____ ____

3. Relates words and pictures.   ____ ____ ____ ____

4. Retells stories in proper sequence.   ____ ____ ____ ____

5. Describes simple objects.   ____ ____ ____ ____

6. Repeats a sentence with 80 percent accuracy.   ____ ____ ____ ____

7. Makes story predictions based on a title or an illustration.   ____ ____ ____ ____

II. Speech-to-Print Match

1. Points to written words as they are read aloud.   ____ ____ ____ ____

2a. Indicates where printed message begins on page.   ____ ____ ____ ____

2b. (DLTA only) Indicates that print and not picture contains message.   ____ ____ ____ ____

3a. Indicates directional orientation of print (left to right).   ____ ____ ____ ____

3b. (DLTA only) Indicates directional orientation of book (front to back).   ____ ____ ____ ____

4. Knows some words in isolation.   ____ ____ ____ ____

5. Recognizes own name in print.   ____ ____ ____ ____

*DA = Developing Adequately.
 NE = Needs More Experiences.

	Obs. I Date _____		Obs. II Date _____	
	DA	NE	DA	NE
III. Letter and Word Recognition				
1. Identifies lowercase letters.	____	____	____	____
2. Identifies uppercase letters.	____	____	____	____
3. Matches two words.	____	____	____	____
4. Matches simple concept words to pictures.	____	____	____	____
IV. Auditory Discrimination Skills				
1. Identifies rhyming words.	____	____	____	____
2. Differentiates beginning letter sounds.	____	____	____	____
3. Differentiates ending letter sounds.	____	____	____	____
V. Visual Motor Skills				
1. Traces letters using left-to-right movement.	____	____	____	____
2. Copies own name using a model.	____	____	____	____

Interpretation and Recommendations

_____

_____

_____

_____

_____

_____

_____

_____

ACTIVITY

USING THE OBSERVATION CHECKLIST
EMERGENT LITERACY STAGE

The following activity provides practice in interpreting observation notes. The information given includes a student's dictated story and a teacher's observation record. The teacher recorded notes on the first two areas of the Observation Checklist (oral language and speech-to-print match), thus, only those areas of the form are provided.

Directions: Read the following scenario and review the completed two sections of the Observation Checklist. Then answer the questions that follow.

Sally is a first-grade child who attended kindergarten. She was observed in September (Obs. I), and her teacher believed her behavior indicated she was shy and did not like working in groups. She also thought Sally had had limited experiences with books. The teacher has been using a whole language approach to reading with **big books** and language experience stories. It is now October. The teacher formed a small group that included Sally and lead a discussion on the students' best-liked experiences in first grade so far. Each child was then asked to dictate an individual story to the teacher. Sally dictated the following:

> I love first grade. It is neat to be learning to read like my brother. My teacher is the best in the whole world. I like my school.

Sally then read the story orally to the teacher, pointing to each word as she read. She then copied it and drew an illustration. Sally's teacher completed the observation form at the conclusion of the lesson, adding the new information (Obs. II).

OBSERVATION CHECKLIST
EMERGENT LITERACY STAGE

Student __Sally__   Grade __1__

Examiner __Cohen__

	Obs. I		Obs. II	
	Date 9/10/93		Date 10/25/93	
	DA*	NE*	DA*	NE*
I. Oral Language Skills				
1. Participates freely in group discussions.	___	✓	___	✓
2. Speaks in complete sentences.	✓	___	✓	___

*DA = Developing Adequately.
 NE = Needs More Experiences.

	Obs. I Date *9/10/93*		Obs. II Date *10/25/93*	
	DA	**NE**	**DA**	**NE**
3. Relates words and pictures.	——	✓	✓	——
4. Retells stories in proper sequence.	——	✓	*not obs.**	
5. Describes simple objects.	*not obs.*		*not obs.*	
6. Repeats a sentence with 80 percent accuracy.	*not obs.*		*not obs.*	
7. Makes story predictions based on a title or an illustration.	——	✓	*not obs.*	

II. Speech-to-Print Match

	DA	NE	DA	NE
1. Points to written words as they are read aloud.	——	✓	✓	——
2a. Indicates where printed message begins on page.	✓	——	✓	——
2b. (DLTA only) Indicates that print and not picture contains message.	✓	——	✓	——
3a. Indicates directional orientation of print (left to right).	✓	——	✓	——
3b. (DLTA only) Indicates directional orientation of book (front to back).	——	✓	✓	——
4. Knows some words in isolation.	✓	——	✓	——
5. Recognizes own name in print.	✓	——	✓	——

Questions

1. What conclusions can you make about Sally based on the observation form completed by the teacher?

2. What additional information would you like to have on Sally?

3. What type of reading instructional program might be most appropriate for Sally?

*not observed

STRUCTURED OBSERVATION OF THE EARLY AND FLUENT LITERACY STAGES

The two structured observation forms that make up the *Observation Checklists: Early and Fluent Literacy Stages* for oral reading and comprehension given in this chapter are recommended for use with children in the early and fluent literacy stages of reading. The Oral and Silent Reading Behaviors Form examines observable behaviors such as the child's pronunciation of words, **self-corrections**, and substitutions during oral reading. The Reading Comprehension Skills Form focuses on the levels of literal, **inferential, creative,** and **critical comprehension**. Combined with an interview to discern a student's reading strategies, these observation forms can provide a starting point for teachers to develop tentative hypotheses from which to make instructional decisions.

Using the Observation Checklists: Early and Fluent Literacy Stages

The purpose of the *Observation Checklists: Early and Fluent Literacy Stsges* is to provide a structured means to observe one child who has reached at least a grade 1 or 1-1 basal reading level.

Preparing for the Observation

Arrange for one of the following situations in which to observe a child:

1. small group reading lesson with a basal text, literature selection, or content textbook
2. individual reading lesson using a basal text, literature selection, or content textbook

You will need a prepared set of comprehension questions to accompany the reading material in order to measure some of the skills listed on the comprehension form. If using a basal text, the questions can be selected from those in the teacher's manual. However, you must be sure to include enough questions at each level of comprehension to make an accurate evaluation. Not all comprehension skills need to be measured at one sitting.

Recording the Observation Data

Record the date of the first observation under the heading Obs. I (Observation I), the second under Obs. II (Observation II). Using the key DA = Developing Adequately or NE = Needs More Experiences, evaluate the child's responses. If you believe the child is developing adequately in the area indicated on the form, place a check in the DA column. If you believe the child needs more work in the area, place a check in the NE column. Record additional comments on the back of the sheet.

For example, if a child was observed on two occasions, the top of the form would look like the following:

Student _Brian_   Grade _3_

Examiner _S. Fisher_

	Obs. I Date _10/12/93_		Obs. II Date _11/15/93_	
	DA	**NE**	**DA**	**NE**
I. Word Identification / Cue Usage				
1. Pronounces basic **sight words** in isolation.	✓	___	✓	___
2. Pronounces basic sight words in **context**.	✓	___	✓	___
3. Uses **phonic principles** in decoding unknown words.	___	✓	___	✓
4. Decodes using **morphemic units** in words.	___	✓	___	✓

OBSERVATION CHECKLIST
EARLY AND FLUENT LITERACY STAGES
ORAL AND SILENT READING BEHAVIORS

Student _____   Grade _____

Examiner _____

	Obs. I		Obs. II	
	Date _____		Date _____	
	DA*	NE*	DA*	NE*
I. Word Identification / Cue Usage				
1. Pronounces basic sight words in isolation.	____	____	____	____
2. Pronounces basic sight words in context.	____	____	____	____
3. Uses phonic principles in decoding unknown words.	____	____	____	____
4. Decodes using morphemic units in words.	____	____	____	____
5. Decodes words using **syllabic units** rather than individual letter sounds.	____	____	____	____
6. Uses context to read unfamiliar words.	____	____	____	____
7. Retains meaning of deviations from text.	____	____	____	____
8. Notes miscues if they interfere with meaning and self-corrects.	____	____	____	____
II. Oral Reading Behaviors (on practiced materials)				
1. Uses appropriate phrasing.	____	____	____	____
2. Holds book correctly.	____	____	____	____
3. Keeps place while reading.	____	____	____	____
4. Reads punctuation correctly.	____	____	____	____

*DA = Developing Adequately.

NE = Needs More Experiences.

	Obs. I Date _____		Obs. II Date _____	
	DA	**NE**	**DA**	**NE**
5. Reads fluently.	____	____	____	____
6. Uses expression.	____	____	____	____

III. Silent Reading Behaviors

1. Holds book correctly.	____	____	____	____
2. Appears to apply reading strategies/ skills independently (does not ask for help often).	____	____	____	____
3. Stays on task.	____	____	____	____
4. Reads at an appropriate rate.	____	____	____	____

Interpretation and Recommendations

_____

_____

_____

_____

_____

_____

_____

_____

_____

_____

_____

OBSERVATION CHECKLIST
EARLY AND FLUENT LITERACY STAGES
READING COMPREHENSION SKILLS

Student _____   Grade _____

Examiner _____

	Obs. I Date _____		Obs. II Date _____	
	DA*	NE*	DA*	NE*
I. Literal Comprehension				
1. States main idea.	____	____	____	____
2. Recalls details.	____	____	____	____
3. Recalls sequence of events.	____	____	____	____
4. Recalls cause-and-effect relationships.	____	____	____	____
5. Identifies setting in a **narrative story**.	____	____	____	____
6. Recalls comparisons and contrasts.	____	____	____	____
7. Retells story with accuracy.	____	____	____	____
8. Describes main character(s).	____	____	____	____
II. Inferential Comprehension				
1. Infers main idea from the passage.	____	____	____	____
2. Draws conclusions/generalizations.	____	____	____	____
3. Interprets figurative language.	____	____	____	____
4. Predicts outcomes; hypothesizes.	____	____	____	____
5. Interprets pictures or illustrations.	____	____	____	____
6. Identifies character traits from story clues.	____	____	____	____
7. Recognizes mood of the story.	____	____	____	____

*DA = Developing Adequately.

NE = Needs More Experiences.

	DA	NE	DA	NE
8. Determines word meanings from context.	——	——	——	——
9. Summarizes major events or points.	——	——	——	——
10. Draws on previous knowledge.	——	——	——	——

III. Critical Comprehension

	DA	NE	DA	NE
1. Differentiates fantasy from fact.	——	——	——	——
2. Differentiates fact from opinion.	——	——	——	——
3. Evaluates character motives and actions.	——	——	——	——
4. Evaluates writing based on personal tastes.	——	——	——	——
5. Questions factual information.	——	——	——	——

IV. Responds to Literature

	DA	NE	DA	NE
1. Develops a new ending for a story.	——	——	——	——
2. Rewrites story using same pattern of language.	——	——	——	——
3. Dramatizes scene from story (puppets, skit, etc.).	——	——	——	——
4. Creates an audiovisual representation of story.	——	——	——	——
5. Develops a semantic map, etc.	——	——	——	——

Interpretation and Recommendations

_____

_____

_____

_____

_____

SAMPLE
Observation: Early and Fluent Literacy Stages

The following is an example of a completed observation of the child's oral and silent reading behaviors with interpretation and recommendations.

Mark was a new student in mid-January who transferred from another state; he brought a minimum amount of information to his teacher. The class had just completed the 2-1 basal reader and had begun the 2-2 reader, so Mark's teacher decided to place him on grade level with his classmates. Mark was observed during reading in January just after his arrival. The teacher observed him again at the end of February.

Student _Mark_   Grade _2_

Examiner _M. Mars_

	Obs. I		Obs. II	
	Date _1/20/93_		Date _2/26/93_	
	DA*	NE*	DA*	NE*

I. Word Identification / Cue Usage

1. Pronounces basic sight words in isolation.	✓	___	✓	___
2. Pronounces basic sight words in context.	✓	___	✓	___
3. Uses phonic principles in decoding unknown words.	✓	___	✓	___
4. Decodes using morphemic units in words.	✓	___	✓	___
5. Decodes words using syllabic units rather than individual letter sounds.	✓	___	✓	___
6. Uses context to read unfamiliar words.	✓	___	✓	___
7. Retains meaning of deviations from text.	✓	___	✓	___
8. Notes miscues if they interfere with meaning and self-corrects.	_did not self-correct_	___	_no self-corrections_	___

*DA = Developing Adequately.

 NE = Needs More Experiences.

	Obs. I Date _1/20/93_		Obs. II Date _2/26/93_	
	DA	NE	DA	NE
II. Oral Reading Behaviors (on practiced materials)				
1. Uses appropriate phrasing.	___	✓	___	✓
2. Holds book correctly.	✓	___	✓	___
3. Keeps place while reading.	✓	___	✓	___
4. Reads punctuation correctly.	___	✓	✓	___
5. Reads fluently.	___	✓	___	✓
6. Uses expression.	___	✓	___	✓
III. Silent Reading Behaviors				
1. Holds book correctly.	✓	___	✓	___
2. Appears to apply reading strategies/skills independently (does not ask for help often).	___	✓	___	✓
3. Stays on task.	___	✓	___	✓
4. Reads at an appropriate rate.	_not obs._		_not obs._	

Interpretation and Recommendations

The observation form covers two sessions—January 20 and February 26. On the initial observation, Mark's oral reading was characterized by incorrect phrasing and a lack of fluency and expression. Mark also ignored punctuation marks as signals. This could have contributed to the improper phrasing. Mark did not self-correct his errors. However, the teacher noted that he substituted words with similar meanings. Thus, self-correction may not have been necessary if meaning was maintained. Further analysis is necessary to determine Mark's comprehension strategies and reading level. On the second observation, Mark was attending more to punctuation, and his phrasing had shown improvement.

Mark's word-identification skills were adequate for his grade placement, according to the teacher. He also seemed to apply basic phonic principles while decoding unknown words. On the initial observation, Mark appeared to use context clues to decode unfamiliar words, borne out by his substitution of similar-meaning words. This was, obviously, one of Mark's strengths. However, when reading silently, Mark did not stay on task and frequently asked for the teacher's help. This behavior had not improved on the second observation. The teacher should work on developing Mark's independent reading habits and provide more opportunities for silent reading with high-interest reading materials.

A C T I V I T Y

USING THE OBSERVATION CHECKLISTS
EARLY AND FLUENT LITERACY STAGES

Directions: Using one or more of the observation forms, observe a child in the early and fluent literacy stages in a natural reading setting. Record the information as instructed, write an interpretation, and give at least one recommendation.

THE INTERVIEW

The person most involved in the diagnostic process is the student. It is interesting to see how the student's perceptions of his or her reading skills are different from those of the teacher and even of his or her parents. The purpose of the interview is to get acquainted with the student and to get a feeling for the student's "life space" (McGinnis & Smith, 1982).

A student's interview responses can reveal feelings about reading and reading instruction, strategies used in reading, and an overall self-assessment. The oral interview is conducted in an informal setting. The student should *not* be given the interview questions as a paper-pencil exercise.

The teacher/interviewer needs to assure the student of confidentiality in order to establish a trusting atmosphere. Without the child's trust or an environment where free exchanges can take place, the interview may provide false or misleading information.

As with observation, the teacher needs a clear objective. The interview can center on the child's attitudes toward school, reading, the self, or his or her reading strategies. It is important that a set of questions be established in advance to guide the interview.

A sample interview follows. Questions may be added to these, but caution should be taken to not make the interview too long. It is advisable to probe a student's response when clarity or further information is desired. For example, if a student responds with "sound it out" to the question "What do you do when you come to a word you do not know?" an appropriate probe might be "Tell me how you do that," or "Where do you start sounding out?"

The age of the student may dictate the language and even the content of the questions. The teacher may want to have a book handy so a child can demonstrate his or her techniques and strategies.

Remember that the purpose of the interview is to learn from the child. This is not intended to be a psychological interview but, rather, one that will provide insight into the child's reading world.

SAMPLE: Interview

The following is a sample of an interview with a fourth-grade boy who was experiencing difficulty in school. His teacher believed he had a possible learning disability.

Student _Justin_____ Age _9____ Grade _4_____

Date _10/6/93_____ School _B. T. Washington_____

Examiner _S. Siger_____

1. Do you like to read?   Yes _____   No _X___
   Yes: Why do you like to read?
   No: Why don't you like to read?
   Because it's boring. The stories are boring.

2. Are you a good reader?   Yes _X___ No _____
   Yes: Why do you think so?
   I can read the words. It's easy to read.
   No: With what parts of reading are you having trouble?

3. If you were going to read a story about *sharks*, what would you do first?
   I just start reading on the first page. Sometimes I look at the pictures before I read the words.

4. What do you do when you come to a word you do not know?
   I ask somebody. (Who do you ask?) *The teacher.*
   Do you do anything else?
   No.

5. What do you do when you do not understand what you have read?
   Read it again. (Do you do anything else?) *No. I can understand it most of the time.*

6. Are there some things about reading that you enjoy?
   No.
   Yes: What are they?

7. Are there some things about reading that you don't like? What are they?

    I don't like writing answers. (What do you mean?) *You know, when you have to answer questions after reading a story. They make us write the answers down.*

8. What is the best story or book you have ever read?

    Baseball Collector's Magazine. (Anything else?). *Guinness Book of World Records.*

9. What would you like to learn to make you a better reader?

    I want to learn how to write paragraphs.

10. What is reading?

    It's when you read a book.

11. Can you read without a book?

    Sure. Sign language.

12. Why do people read?

    Because they have to.

    Why do *you* read?

    Because I have to. Somebody told me to read. (What about when you read your magazine on baseball cards?) *Oh, I like to read that. That's for fun.*

Interpretation and Recommendations

This young boy did not enjoy reading that occurred in school. He believed himself to be a good reader even though his teacher saw him as deficient. His reading strategies were somewhat limited, according to the interview. He said he would ask someone if he didn't know a word or read it again if he didn't understand it. This, in fact, was confirmed with additional observation. He was having considerable difficulty with paragraph writing at the time of the interview, thus, his comment about learning how to write paragraphs to be a better reader reflected the current emphasis in classroom instruction. He intuitively previews the reading by looking at pictures, but this may not be a regularly used strategy. More attention to bridging background knowledge before reading is advised. Additional testing revealed the child's instructional reading level to be sixth grade. Instruction should be focused on increasing his interest in reading and providing additional strategies for comprehension.

ACTIVITY

INTERVIEWING

Directions: Using the following sample interview form or developing your own interview questions, interview a student to determine the strategies the student used during reading and his or her attitudes toward reading. Write an interpretation and at least one recommendation.

QUESTIONS FOR INTERVIEWING

Student _____ Age _____ Grade_____

Date _____ School _____

Interviewer _____

1. Do you like to read?   Yes _____   No _____
   Yes: Why do you like to read?
   No: Why don't you like to read?

2. Are you a good reader?   Yes _____   No _____
   Yes: Why do you think so?
   No: With what parts of reading are you having trouble?

3. If you were going to read a story about *sharks*, what would you do first?

4. What do you do when you come to a word you do not know?
   Do you do anything else?

5. What do you do when you do not understand what you have read?

6. Are there some things about reading that you enjoy?
   Yes: What are they?

7. Are there some things about reading that you don't like? What are they?

8. What is the best story or book you have ever read?

9. What would you like to learn to make you a better reader?

10. What is reading?

11. Can you read without a book?

12. Why do people read?
    Why do *you* read?

Interpretation and Recommendations

SUMMARY

In this chapter, you were given a brief overview of structured observations for the emergent and the early and fluent literacy stages. In addition, you were given an interview format for use with students in the early and fluent stages. These two methods of evaluation can provide clues to students' reading and comprehension strategies, oral language, and knowledge of print concepts. All of these areas are essential to the development of the reading process.

SUGGESTED READINGS

Clay, M. M. (1985). *The early detection of reading difficulties* (3rd ed.). Auckland, New Zealand: Heinemann Publishers.

Downing, J., & Thackery, D. (1976). *Reading readiness*. London: Hodder and Stoughton.

Glazer, S., & Searfoss, L. (1988). *Reading diagnosis and instruction: A C-A-L-M approach*. Englewood Cliffs, NJ: Prentice Hall.

Richek, M. A., List, Lynne K., & Lerner, J. W. (1989). *Reading problems: Assessment and teaching strategies* (2nd ed.). Englewood Cliffs, NJ: Prentice Hall.

Rubin, D. (1991). *Diagnosis and correction in reading instruction* (2nd ed.). Boston: Allyn & Bacon.

CHAPTER 4/

USING STANDARDIZED TEST SCORES

This chapter provides experiences with standardized norm-referenced test information. The teacher will find it useful to understand and interpret formal test scores in making instructional decisions. Practice exercises include converting **raw scores** into **standard scores** using a chart similar to that in test manuals, applying the **standard error of measurement (SEM),** and making generalizations and observations about test scores.

After working through this chapter, the importance of using more than just a standardized test score to make any classroom or school decision will be evident. It will also be apparent that if a standardized test score is the only data available on a child, the information is limiting. Standardized test scores have value as one of several sources of information but should not be the only data source on which to base instructional decisions.

INTERPRETING SCORES

The ability to interpret standardized test scores is important in decision making and in evaluating instruction. A thorough understanding of test scores permits a teacher to make informed decisions. It also helps the teacher interpret test scores for parents and students.

A few definitions may be in order:

Raw score: The actual number of items correctly answered on a test.

Derived score: A derived score is a numerical score obtained by converting a raw score using a norm scale. Derived scores provide meaning to raw scores so we can make comparisons. Specific types of derived scores include grade equivalents, percentile ranks, stanines, and normal curve equivalents.

Percentile rank: A percentile rank gives a person's relative position within a defined group. A percentile rank of 30 indicates a person scored as high as or higher than 30 percent of the people in that particular group.

Stanine: A standard score of nine units, 1–9. In a normal distribution, stanines 1–3 indicate below-average performance, 4–6 indicate average performance, and 7–9 indicate above-average performance.

Grade equivalent: A derived score expressed in grade years and months, i.e., 3.5 (third grade, fifth month). Comparison of an individual's grade-equivalent score is made with the subject's norm group. A grade-equivalent score tends to be misinterpreted; thus, its usage in describing a child's achievement level is strongly discouraged.

SAMPLE
Standardized Test Scores Interpretation

The Henry Public School District administers a standardized achievement test every spring. This test covers reading, language, and mathematics. The following table gives five fourth-grade students' scores in reading:

Student	Vocabulary		Comprehension		Total	
	NP*	Stanine	NP*	Stanine	NP*	Stanine
Jean	1	1	9	2	4	1
José	13	3	15	3	14	3
Christopher	85	7	74	6	79	7
Michael	55	5	42	5	47	5
Marcus	28	4	31	4	31	4

*National Percentile.

According to the table, Christopher scored in the upper quartile in vocabulary and total reading. He also achieved in the high-average range in comprehension. Compared to the norm group, Christopher is achieving in the upper third of the fourth-grade students, and his fifth-grade teacher may need to provide challenging tasks for him.

Jean, however, scored in the lower third in all areas of the test. These scores do not indicate in what areas of vocabulary or comprehension Jean has particular weaknesses or strengths. Her fifth-grade teacher will need to examine Jean's needs more carefully and make accommodations in her reading material. Jean may need an alternative basal program (if the basal is the predominant method) or an intensive remedial program.

Marcus appears to be achieving in the low-average range and may need corrective instruction in some areas. A structured vocabulary program may be useful for Marcus. His fifth-grade teacher will need to conduct informal testing to determine his specific needs.

José's scores may reflect a language deficit if he is bilingual. If so, his teacher will need to observe and test him informally to get a truer picture of his level of achievement. A program designed to increase his oral language fluency and reading vocabulary may prove effective.

Michael is achieving well in the average range of reading compared to the norm group. His fifth-grade teacher should expect him to read his fifth-grade material with adequate comprehension.

These standardized test scores give only general indications of a child's level of achievement. Specific needs and strengths cannot be determined on the basis of norm-referenced test scores.

A C T I V I T Y

INTERPRETING STANDARDIZED READINESS TEST SCORES

Directions: The information below is based on results from the *Clymer-Barrett Readiness Test* (1983)[1] administered at the end of the kindergarten year. Examine the data in the table, and answer the questions that follow. Use the guidelines as well as the data to formulate your answers.

Guidelines for Interpreting Test Scores

Stanine	Skill Development
9	Excellent ability in measured skill.
8–7	Good capability in the measured skill. May need further reinforcement.
6–4	Average capability in the measured skill. Continued skill instruction must be carefully evaluated and modified.
3–2	Limited capability in measured skill. Will need exposure and structured practice before a formal reading instruction program can begin.
1	Almost no capacity in measured skill. Intensive instruction is recommended.

[1] Reprinted with permission of Chapman, Brook, and Kent, PO Box 3030, Blue Jay, California, 92317.

Student	Visual Discrimination		Auditory Discrimination		Visual-Motor Coordination		Total	Percentile Rank
	RS*	S*	RS	S	RS	S	S	
Kim	30	4	23	4	12	4	4	34
Jose	43	6	31	5	19	6	6	68
James	21	3	15	2	19	6	4	24
Melissa	38	5	20	3	12	4	4	40
Daren	10	2	16	2	3	1	1	2
Holly	21	3	10	1	10	3	2	7

*RS = Raw Score

S = Stanine

Questions

1. On the basis of only these test scores, which children appear ready for a formal (basal) reading program?

    Why do you say that?

2. Which children need more readiness training, and in what areas?

    Why?

3. If you were the teacher, how would you structure this training?

4. How would you interpret James's scores for his parents?

CONVERTING RAW SCORES

As has been noted, a raw score is the total number of items answered correctly, whereas a derived score is one that is calculated from the raw score and based on a normative scale.

In some instances, the teacher will need to administer a standardized test and supply derived scores for a set of raw scores using a test manual. This task may appear rather elementary; however, correctly locating the appropriate derived scores and recording these scores is an important step to using the information.

A C T I V I T Y

CONVERTING RAW SCORES

The purpose of this task is to practice converting raw scores into stanines, percentile ranks, and grade equivalents using a chart similar to those found in standardized test manuals.

Directions: A standardized reading survey test was administered in September at the Forest School. The results for ten children in Mr. Harris's fifth-grade class are given below. Using the accompanying norm chart, find the percentile rank, stanine, and grade equivalent based on the raw score given for each student and complete the table. Then write a brief interpretation of the students' achievement levels.

Student	Raw Score	Percentile Rank	Stanine	Grade Equivalent
Jimmy	55			
Tim	30			
Becky	61			
Flora	47			
Jennifer	40			
Lou	82			
Hazel	49			
Mark	75			
Randy	34			
Celine	51			

What can you say about the achievement of these students?

Norm Chart—Grade 5

Raw Score	Percentile Rank	Stanine	Grade Equivalent
84–85	99	9	11.0
82–83	98	9	10.9
81	97	9	10.6
79–80	96	8	10.2
78	95	8	9.7
77	94	8	9.5
76	93	8	9.2
75	92	8	9.0
74	90	7	8.6
73	89	7	8.4
72	86	7	8.2
71	86	7	8.0
70	80	7	7.7
69	77	7	7.5
68	75	6	7.2
67	73	6	7.0
66	71	6	6.8
65	69	6	6.6
64	65	6	6.4
63	61	6	6.2
62	58	6	6.0
61	53	5	5.8
60	50	5	5.6

Raw Score	Percentile Rank	Stanine	Grade Equivalent
59	45	5	5.4
58	40	5	5.2
57	36	4	5.0
56	33	4	4.8
55	30	4	4.6
54	27	4	4.4
53	24	4	4.2
51–52	21	3	4.0
50	19	3	3.8
49	17	3	3.6
48	15	3	3.4
46–47	13	3	3.2
44–45	11	3	2.8
43	10	2	2.6
42	9	2	2.4
41	8	2	2.2
40	7	2	2.0
39	6	2	1.8
37–38	5	2	1.6
33–36	4	1	1.4
29–32	3	1	1.2
27–28	2	1	1.0
1–26	1	1	1.0

THE STANDARD ERROR OF MEASUREMENT

The *standard error of measurement (SEM)* indicates how much one would expect a person's score to vary if the same standardized test were given several times. It is one way of expressing a test's reliability. Most often, the SEM is provided in the test manual and, therefore, the teacher does not have to compute it. The SEM can be used to avoid a common misinterpretation that a test score is a "true" score.

Assuming that a person's raw score, or obtained score, is the "true" score can lead to trouble. Every score actually rests within a range. The score achieved on the day of the test represents an estimate of the student's performance on that day and time. The range of score values in which the score falls more accurately reflects a student's actual achievement. The teacher can guard against making errors in judgment or evaluation by utilizing a **confidence level** with which to interpret and evaluate test performance. Using the SEM minimizes the possibility of misinterpretation based on one test score and provides a more rational basis for interpreting test scores.

The SEM estimates the error of an individual's test score. A person's "true" score will fall within a range of plus or minus *one* SEM on either side of the reported score 68 percent of the time. Thus, if a person obtained a score of 35 and the SEM was 5 points, then the range in which his or her "true" score would fall 68 percent of the time would be from 30 to 40. This range is the 68 percent confidence level.

If a range of plus or minus *two* SEM is used, a person's true score would fall within that range approximately 95 percent of the time. So, given the same information as above, the 95 percent confidence level would be from 25 to 45 (35 plus or minus 10). As you can see, the test score range, or band, is broader for the 95 percent confidence level.

┌─────────────────────┐
│ A C T I V I T Y │
└─────────────────────┘

USING THE STANDARD ERROR OF MEASUREMENT

The purpose of this activity is to illustrate the use of the standard error of measurement (SEM) with individuals' reported test scores.

Directions: Below is a chart with the same children from the previous activity. Using the normative information you derived in that activity, determine the test score ranges at the 68 percent confidence level for both the percentile and stanine scores. The standard error of measurement (SEM) is 4.2 on the raw score. Then, using your calculations, answer the questions that follow. Jimmy's scores are done for you.

Confidence Level Test Score Ranges

Student	Raw Score	Raw Score Range		68% Confidence Level Percentile Range	68% Confidence Level Stanine Range
Jimmy	55	50.8	59.2	21–45	3–5
Tim	30				
Becky	61				
Flora	47				
Jennifer	40				
Lou	82				
Hazel	49				
Mark	75				
Randy	34				
Celine	51				

Questions

1. For which students would you like more information? Why?

2. What type of information would you like for each of these students?

3. What conclusions about Tim, Jennifer, Randy, and Lou can you *reasonably* draw from the data?

4. Why is it more effective to give the "true" score range than to give a single score?

5. If Becky's parents wanted you to explain her test results, how would you present the scores and interpret them?

SUMMARY

This chapter included activities using standardized norm-referenced test scores. In addition, you were given experiences with the standard error of measurement and the utilization of test scores in decision making. The interpretation and cautious use of standardized test scores was emphasized throughout the chapter.

SUGGESTED READINGS

Carey, L. (1988). *Measuring and evaluating school learning.* Boston: Allyn & Bacon. Ch. 12.

Farr, R., & Carey, R. F. (1986). *Reading: What can be measured?* (2nd ed.). Newark, NJ: International Reading Association.

Lyman, H. B. (1991). *Test scores and what they mean* (5th ed.). Englewood Cliffs, NJ: Prentice Hall.

5 / IDENTIFYING PROBLEM READERS

Determining that a child has a problem in reading is the first phase of more intensive data gathering, or diagnosis. One piece of information the teacher may wish to uncover is the severity of the observed problem and the type of problem. Traditionally, a **reading expectancy** formula has been used for this purpose.

There are various classifications of readers:

Developmental readers: Those who are progressing normally for their age/grade. Instruction follows the basic program, often a basal reading method.

Corrective readers: Those who have minor deficiencies in one or more skill areas. Corrective instruction is short-term and usually specific to the need.

Remedial readers: Those who have severe problems and perform considerably below their **potential reading level**. Instruction is delivered by a specialist in a small group or individualized setting. Other terms related to problem readers include *disabled readers*.

Be advised that these terms should not be used to label readers as they do not identify the child's special strengths or needs as a learner. However, if used appropriately and if all members of the educational team understand the definitions, these labels can provide insight into the type of educational program that can benefit the child.

A child has a reading problem only if he or she is not reading up to expectancy or potential. To assess the discrepancy between achievement and potential, teachers can use **listening comprehension** tests or reading expectancy formulae. These methods, however, are only estimates and should always be used in conjunction with other data in considering the learner's needs. The teacher must consider the learner's past history of progress, reading behavior over time, and the results of diagnostic measures.

Reading expectancy is determined by using a valid measure of intelligence or a measure of listening comprehension. These scores are then used in a formula that provides an estimate of the child's potential for reading achievement. If the child's actual reading achievement level is significantly below the expected level, then a possible reading problem exists. Thus, grade-level placement, as an indicator of expected reading level, should not be used to determine whether the child is progressing properly. That is, just because a fourth-grader is reading below grade level does not mean the child is "disabled" or "remedial." The child's achievement level must be considered relative to the child's potential reading level not just grade placement.

The activities in this chapter are designed to provide practice in using listening comprehension scores and reading expectancy formulae to determine if a child has a reading problem. In addition, one activity, interviewing a school specialist, will help you review the procedures used in schools to identify and place students in remedial or special programs.

LISTENING COMPREHENSION

Listening comprehension is the highest level at which a child can listen and satisfactorily comprehend connected discourse (usually with 70 percent accuracy). Listening comprehension is often considered a measure of aptitude and may be more educationally relevant than traditional IQ tests.

There are several ways to determine listening comprehension. Some standardized tests contain a listening subtest. The teacher can use informal reading inventories (IRI), discussed in Chapter 6, or graded passages from the student's instructional materials with accompanying comprehension questions. With the latter two methods, the teacher reads a selection aloud to the child and asks questions. The process continues with progressively harder passages until the child comprehends with less than 70 percent accuracy.

To evaluate whether a discrepancy between potential and achievement exists, the highest listening comprehension level achieved by the child is converted to a **listening age** by adding 5.2 to the grade level of the passage. For example, Peter, a fourth-grader, scored at the 4.1 grade-equivalent level in listening comprehension on the *Stanford Achievement Test*. To determine his listening age, add 5.2 to 4.1.

listening age = listening comprehension grade + 5.2

listening age = 4.1 + 5.2 = 9.3

His listening age is then compared with his **reading age**. This is computed by adding 5.2 to his reading achievement grade-equivalent score, which was 3.0.

reading age = reading achievement grade + 5.2

reading age = 3.0 + 5.2 = 8.2

There is a discrepancy between Peter's potential (listening age 9.3) and his actual achievement (reading age 8.2).

In contrast, Melody, also a fourth-grader, has a listening comprehension grade of 3.5 and reading achievement grade of 3.0. When her listening and reading ages are compared, there is little discrepancy.

listening age = 3.5 + 5.2 = 8.7

reading age = 3.0 + 5.2 = 8.2

Both Peter and Melody have the same reading achievement level. However, Peter is demonstrating a greater discrepancy in achievement versus potential, whereas Melody is achieving at her potential. Thus, even though they are both achieving below their grade placement, Peter is considered to have a reading problem and Melody is not.

There are limitations to using listening comprehension as a measure of expectancy. Children who have auditory handicaps, are bilingual, or have delayed language development may have low listening comprehension scores and indicate a lower potential than actually exists. In these cases, listening comprehension is probably invalid, and other measures of potential should be employed.

ACTIVITY

USING LISTENING COMPREHENSION TESTS

Directions: Below are four fifth-grade students' scores on the listening comprehension subtest and reading comprehension subtest of a standardized achievement test. Determine which children have a potential reading problem by calculating their listening and reading ages and comparing the two scores.

Student	Listening		Reading	
	GE*	NP*	GE*	NP*
Ricardo	4.4	25	5.6	46
Karen	2.4	3	2.9	8
Bridgette	5.2	38	2.7	5
Alyssa	4.4	25	3.3	14

*GE = Grade Equivalent.

NP = National Percentile.

READING EXPECTANCY QUOTIENT
AND READING QUOTIENT

The degree and nature of a reading problem can be estimated by using reading expectancy formulae recommended by Harris and Sipay (1990), which you can consult for a full explanation. This procedure uses a ratio, or quotient, in comparing a student's expected level of achievement with his or her actual level of achievement.

Harris and Sipay (1990) developed the following formulae to determine if a reading problem exists. Reading age is a measure of a child's reading achievement derived by adding 5.2 to a grade equivalent score obtained from a reading achievement test. **Reading expectancy age (R Exp A)** relates a child's mental age (intelligence) to his or her chronological age. This provides a measure of the child's anticipated, or potential, reading performance. Once the R Exp A is determined, it can be used to compare anticipated reading achievement to actual reading performance and also to chronological age. The former comparison is termed **reading expectancy quotient** and the latter is **reading quotient**.

Procedure for Determining a Reading Problem

Step 1   Compute the reading age (RA) by adding 5.2 to the student's reading grade-equivalent score.

reading age (RA) = reading grade + 5.2

Step 2   Convert the chronological age (CA) into decimals using the following conversion chart.

Conversion Chart from Chronological Age Months to Decimals (tenths)

1 month = .1 of a year

2 months = .2 of a year

3 months = .25 of a year

4 months = .3 of a year

5 months = .4 of a year

6 months = .5 of a year

7 months = .6 of a year

8 months = .7 of a year

9 months = .75 of a year

10 months = .8 of a year

11 months = .9 of a year

For example, if a child is 10 years 8 months of age, the conversion would be 10.7 because 8 months converts to .7. If the mental age (MA) has not been given, compute the MA from the reported IQ. Then convert the MA into decimals using the conversion chart.

$$\text{mental age (MA)} = \frac{CA \times IQ}{100}$$

Step 3   Compute the reading expectancy age (R Exp A).

$$\text{reading expectancy age (R Exp A)} = \frac{2MA + CA}{3}$$

Step 4   Compute the reading expectancy quotient (R Exp Q).

$$\text{reading expectancy quotient (R Exp Q)} = \frac{RA \times 100}{R \; Exp \; A}$$

Step 5   Compute the reading quotient (RQ).

$$\text{reading quotient (RQ)} = \frac{RA \times 100}{CA}$$

Step 6   Determine the type of reader by analyzing the results based on the score ranges provided in the following chart.

If R Exp Q is	and the RQ is	Possible Indications
90–100	>90	Child is a normal reader.
90–100	<90	Child is reading at expectancy but has limited potential.
85–89	>90	Child is an underachiever.
<85	<90	Child has a reading disability.

Example

The following is an example of how to determine if a reading problem exists using the reading expectancy quotient and reading quotient.

Kevin is in third grade reading at 2.4 reading level. He is 8 years 2 months old and has never been retained. His reported IQ is 115 on the WISC-R. Does Kevin have a possible reading problem, and if so, what type of problem is indicated?

Step 1   RA = 2.4 + 5.2 = 7.6

Step 2   CA = 8.2 (in years and months), which is 8.2 in years and tenths

$$MA = \frac{8.2 \times 115}{100} = \frac{943}{100} = 9.43 \text{ (in years and months)}$$

MA = 9.3 (in years and tenths)

Step 3 $R \; Exp \; A = \frac{2(9.3) + 8.2}{3} = \frac{26.8}{3} = 8.93$

Step 4 $$\text{R Exp Q} = \frac{7.6 \times 100}{8.93} = \frac{760}{8.93} = 85.11$$

Step 5 $$\text{RQ} = \frac{7.6 \times 100}{8.2} = \frac{760}{8.2} = 92.68$$

Step 6 Kevin has a possible reading problem because his R Exp Q is in the 85–89 range. This indicates he is not reading up to expectancy. Kevin is most probably an underachiever in that his RQ is above 90, indicating that his reading skill is close to his grade age. He may have some problems but can probably keep up with his school assignments.

> ## A C T I V I T Y

DETERMINING PROBLEM READERS USING READING EXPECTANCY QUOTIENT AND READING QUOTIENT

Directions: Below are data on five children. Determine their reading age, mental age, reading expectancy age, reading expectancy quotient, and reading quotient, and summarize the results for each child as done in the preceding example. Follow the steps on page 60 and complete the information below.

Student	CA	IQ	Reading Grade-equivalent Score	Grade Placement
Denise	12.5	85	5.2	7
Stephanie	15.7	110	9.0	10
David	7.9	135	2.5	2
Bob	10.0	118	4.4	5
Harold	8.3	95	2.5	3

Student	RA	MA	R Exp A	R Exp Q	RQ
Denise					
Stephanie					
David					
Bob					
Harold					

DEGREE OF TOLERABLE DIFFERENCE

Another method of determining whether a child has a possible reading problem is the *degree of tolerable difference* proposed by Wilson and Cleland (1985). With this method, the reading expectancy age is computed and then subtracted from the reading age. This provides a score comparing the difference between potential and achievement. Before selecting children for remediation, however, the child's grade level is taken into consideration, and Wilson provides guidelines for "tolerable differences" between potential and achievement. That is, when a student's difference score is greater than the degree of tolerable difference, the child should be referred for further diagnosis and remediation.

Formulae and Guidelines

Formulae

1. reading age (RA) = reading grade + 5.2

2. mental age (MA) = $\dfrac{CA \times IQ}{100}$ (CA = chronological age)

3. reading expectancy age (R Exp A) = $\dfrac{2\,MA + CA}{3}$

Guidelines

If the child is at the end of grade:	The allowable tolerable difference (in years):
1–3	.5
4–6	1
7–9	1.5
10–l2	2

Example

The following is an example of how to determine a reading problem using the degree of tolerable difference:

Peggy is in eighth grade. Her reading achievement score on a standardized test is 7.2. Peggy's IQ is given at 105 and her chronological age is 14.3.

1. RA = 7.2 + 5.2 = 12.4

2. MA = $\dfrac{14.3 \times 105}{100}$ = 15.01

3. R Exp A = $\dfrac{2(15.01) + 14.3}{3}$ = 14.77

The difference between Peggy's potential and achievement is = 14.77 − 12.4 = 2.37

Peggy's expectancy age is 2 years greater than her actual achievement age. This 2-year difference is outside the tolerable range for her age and grade level (see guidelines). She should be referred for further testing.

ACTIVITY

USING THE DEGREE OF TOLERABLE DIFFERENCE

Directions: Below are data for five children. Determine which children have a possible reading problem using the child's reading age (RA), mental age (MA), reading expectancy age (R Exp A), and degree of tolerable difference guidelines. Decide whether the children with problems should be referred for further testing.

Student	CA	IQ	Reading Grade-equivalent Score	Grade Placement
Harry	10.8	90	4.0	5
Rick	16.9	108	9.5	11
Margie	8.2	140	3.5	3
Carol	9.4	78	1.7	4
Andrea	7.6	99	1.0	2

Student	RA	MA	R Exp A	Difference	Referral (Y/N)
Harry					
Rick					
Margie					
Carol					
Andrea					

INTERVIEW OF A READING SPECIALIST

The purposes of this activity are to:

1. acquaint you with the processes and tools of diagnosis utilized in a school.
2. discover how children with reading problems are identified.
3. determine how screening information is translated for the classroom teacher in the instructional program.

To conduct this task, arrange an interview with either a school reading specialist or learning disabilities teacher (or both).

A list of suggested questions is provided here for your interview; however, you are encouraged to develop additional questions. After the interview, compile the information in one of the following ways to report your findings:

1. Write a summary report of the interview(s).
2. Write a comparison/contrast report of the two specialists' methods.
3. Write an evaluation of the diagnostic process from the perspective of a classroom teacher.
4. Write an evaluation of the diagnostic process from the perspective of a parent.
5. Develop a written list of tests and materials used by the specialist(s).
6. Report orally to the class on any of the above.

Suggested Interview Questions

1. How do you become aware of a child who needs help in school?
2. What is expected of the classroom teacher prior to a referral?
3. How is the parent involved in the evaluation?
4. What are the criteria for selecting children for evaluation and special programs?
5. What diagnostic tests do you use? What other materials or equipment do you use in a diagnosis?
6. How much importance is placed on the yearly standardized group tests in selecting children for special programs?
7. Who's decision is the final authority for selecting children for special programs? How is that decision made?
8. What assistance is given to the regular classroom teacher for implementing suggested procedures/activities once a child has been diagnosed?
9. What assistance is given to parents in implementing changes in the home to help the child's learning?

10. If a child is a "borderline" case and is having difficulty in the classroom, what do you do?
11. What is the most common problem you see in children?
12. If you could change your role in any way, what would it be?

Your questions:

_____

_____

_____

_____

_____

_____

_____

_____

_____

_____

_____

_____

_____

_____

_____

_____

_____

_____

_____

SUMMARY

Being able to determine if a child has a reading problem is more complex than examining test scores. You learned that one method for determining whether a reading problem exists is to compare the child's achievement with his or her potential. Listening comprehension, reading expectancy, and the degree of tolerable difference are viable methods for you to use in the classroom when determining the type and degree of a student's reading problem.

SUGGESTED READINGS

Bond, G. L., Tinker, M. A., Wasson, B. B., & Wasson, J. B. (1989). *Reading difficulties: Their diagnosis and correction* (6th ed.). Englewood Cliffs, NJ: Prentice Hall.

Gillet, J., & Temple, C. (1990). *Understanding reading problems* (3rd ed.). Glenview, IL: Scott, Foresman/Little, Brown.

Harris, A. J., & Sipay, E. R. (1990). *How to increase reading ability: A guide to developmental and remedial methods* (9th ed.). White Plains, NY: Longman.

Rubin, D. (1991). *Diagnosis and correction in reading instruction* (2nd ed.). Boston: Allyn & Bacon.

CHAPTER 6/

INFORMAL READING INVENTORY

An essential premise of assessment, one observed by most successful teachers, is that it is continuous. Thus, every teacher-pupil interaction has the potential to be an assessment event. The teacher can observe the student informally during any type of reading activity. Guided and independent practice exercises as well as informally administered tests can serve as assessment tools.

Diagnosis is more intensive and requires a one-to-one, teacher-student, interaction. The activities in this chapter concentrate on the initial phase of the diagnostic process. This chapter deals first with the mechanics of administering and scoring an **informal reading inventory (IRI);** then it addresses the interpretation of a student's responses on an IRI through the **quantitative** and **qualitative analysis** of errors.

It is our experience that the IRI provides the most complete and useful information about readers. In some schools, teachers administer an IRI to every child at the start of the year primarily to determine reading levels. An indepth analysis of a student's responses on an IRI provides information for the diagnostic process.

Whatever the teacher's model of reading, an IRI gives the type of information required to provide curricular modification, classroom adaptations, and/or remedial corrective instruction. The IRI is nonstandardized, individually administered, and consists of a series of graded passages, each with accompanying comprehension questions. There are usually two comparable passages for each grade level. Some IRIs contain a word-recognition test that may be used to determine the level at which to begin testing.

One of the major reasons for administering an IRI is to determine a student's **independent, instructional,** and **frustration reading levels.** Reading levels are determined by quantitative analysis, which consists of counting the number of errors in word recognition and comprehension and evaluating those numbers according to standard criteria. From this information, the teacher can group students for instruction and provide appropriate-level materials for independent reading. Generally, a student's independent reading level is considered the level at which recreational reading and homework should take place. The student reads with ease, needs little or no teacher assistance, and maintains maximum comprehension. A student's instructional reading level is that at which instruction, or teaching, should take place. At this level, the material is challenging for the student yet not too difficult in either word recognition or comprehension. The teacher generally needs to prepare the reader by preteaching vocabulary and guiding the reading. The student's frustration reading level is that level on which the student has a great deal of difficulty in pronouncing words and in understanding the content. The material at this level is too difficult for the student and is not appropriate for instruction or pleasure reading.

The IRI also allows for observation of the strategies the student uses in approaching the reading task. For example, a student may pronounce words accurately but not know the meaning of the word or lose the meaning of the entire passage. This student may be proficient at "word calling" because he or she has strong word-identification strategies but may lack the needed comprehension strategies. Another student may mispronounce many words in a passage and make many substitutions but comprehend what was read. This student may be a "contextual reader" or may have a strong schema. By employing qualitative analysis of the strategies used, the teacher has a basis on which to form hypotheses concerning a student's needs. The IRI provides the vehicle for such structured observation and qualitative analysis.

ADMINISTRATION OF THE INFORMAL READING INVENTORY

An IRI may be either teacher-made or commercially published. The administration of the IRI passages is the same for both types. It usually takes from 15 to 30 minutes to give an IRI to one child. Because the IRI is individually administered, it is very important for the teacher to establish rapport with the student. The room should be free from distractions and noise, and the environment should be comfortable for both the student and the teacher.

Step 1: Determining a Starting Point

To determine a starting point, most published IRIs begin with the administration of a graded word list. Generally, the initial word list presented is two grade levels below the student's current grade placement. Based on the number correctly pronounced, the manual will suggest a starting point for the reading passages.

If the teacher is using a teacher-made IRI and/or there are no word lists, the teacher may use past records, current reading level, or some other informal reading assessment to determine the level of the starting passage. It is often advisable to begin with reading passages one or two levels below the highest reported norm-referenced grade-equivalent score. If no information is available on the student, administration of the reading passages should begin two levels below the current grade placement.

Step 2: Assessing Oral Reading and Comprehension of Connected Text

The teacher provides the student with a copy of the reading passage determined as a starting point in Step 1. The teacher explains that the student will read the passage orally and that when the student is finished, the teacher will ask questions on the reading. While the student reads, the teacher marks all oral reading errors. The teacher should not give assistance in decoding a word. However, if a student stops reading for 5 to 10 seconds or asks for help, the teacher may pronounce the word.

After the student has read the entire passage, the teacher removes it from the student's sight and asks the comprehension questions, noting the student's responses. The student is not allowed to look back in the text for the answers. It is appropriate for the teacher to ask the child to "Tell me more" or to "Explain" an answer if the student's response is incomplete or vague.

Teachers may use a stopwatch to assess reading rate. It is also permissible to use a tape recorder, but the teacher still needs to mark all word-recognition errors and comprehension responses at the time of testing to determine when to stop administering reading passages.

The teacher continues administering higher grade-level passages until the student reaches the frustration level on comprehension or on both word recognition and comprehension. In some cases, a student will not frustrate in comprehension but will reach the frustration level in word recognition. The teacher can continue testing until the frustration level is reached in both areas. However, *this is a judgment call.* The teacher must evaluate the student at all times and note emotional reactions as well as the quantitative responses during testing.

At this point in the administration of the IRI, both the instructional and frustration reading levels should have been determined. If the student reads the first passage orally at either the instructional or frustration reading levels, lower passages should be administered (if possible) to determine the independent reading level. While the determination of all three levels is desirable, finding the instructional level is particularly important as it provides key information in the match between student and reading material.

Step 3: Assessing Silent Reading Level

Once the oral frustration reading level is determined, the teacher then provides passages for the student to read silently. Most commercial IRIs provide three parallel forms, so one of these alternate forms may be used to assess the silent instructional level. Again, the teacher may use a stopwatch to determine silent reading rate. The administration of the silent reading passages begins at the previously determined oral reading instructional level. When the student completes the reading, the teacher removes the passage from view and asks the comprehension questions. Silent reading is discontinued when the student reaches a frustration level in comprehension.

Step 4: Assessing Listening Comprehension Level

The determination of a listening comprehension level is sometimes considered optional. Begin testing for listening comprehension with the passage one level higher than the instruction level obtained on the silent reading portion of the IRI. The teacher reads the passage orally and then asks the comprehension questions. Testing is discontinued at the listening level when the student comprehends with less than 70 percent accuracy.

RECORDING OF ORAL READING ERRORS

The teacher records oral reading errors and answers to comprehension questions during the administration of an IRI. In addition, observable behaviors related to the reading act, such as finger pointing, head moving, squinting, etc., and behaviors indicating frustration, such as lack of fluency, vocal tension, and reluctance to initiate or complete the task, should be written on the test protocols in the Comments section.

There are eight oral reading errors usually recorded during an IRI. Published IRIs provide guidelines on the types of errors that are counted as quantitative data. The eight errors listed and described below are always recorded. There is a difference, however, in whether and when to include repetitions as quantitative data. If using the Betts criteria, the teacher should consider repetitions as errors; if using the Powell criteria, the teacher should not (see the next section on analyzing quantitative data). In the latter situation, repetitions are used for qualitative analysis. Self-corrections never count as "errors." They do, however, provide valuable hints to the student's reading strategies.

Types of errors, their definitions, and a system for marking them on the reading passage follow:

Miscue Errors	Description	Marking
Substitution	Student replaces a word or phrase with another word or phrase.	*back* in the ~~park~~
Omission	Student skips one or more words in the text.	in the (park)
Addition/insertion	Student adds one or more words to the passage.	*big* in the ‸ park
Mispronunciation	Student incorrectly pronounces or sounds out a word or part of a word.	*perk* in the ~~park~~
Reversal	Student transposes adjacent words or sounds within a word.	(in the) park
Words aided	Student makes no attempt to pronounce word within 10 seconds, and the teacher supplies the word.	*A* in the park
Repetition*	Student repeats two or more consecutive words in the text.	←——— in the park
Self-correction†	Student spontaneously corrects an error.	*sc* *perk* in the park

*Repetitions are scored with Betts criteria but are recorded only with the Powell criteria.

†Self-corrections are recorded but not scored as errors.

The following is a sample of a passage with recorded errors:

Pirates sailed the seas many years ago. Pirates hunted and ~~stole~~ *sold*

treasures on land and on the sea~~s~~ *the* (.)

Men ~~would~~ *could* become pirates to get rich. As sailors, men were paid

low wages and conditions were ~~usually~~ *unusual* poor on a ship. *candids sc*

Pirates often
Pirating offered men a chance to get rich quick~~ly~~ As pirates, they

~~shared~~ *shored* in "the loot."

MARKING AND CLASSIFYING ORAL READING ERRORS

The purpose of this activity is to practice marking and classifying oral reading errors during an IRI.

Directions: Examine each of the oral reading responses given by a child on an IRI, and classify the behavior according to the chart on page 72 following the model of the three examples given below. Some of the items in this activity may have more than one error classification. Then, mark the first column ("Text Word") as you would during an IRI testing.

Text Word	Student's Response	Classification
~~mother~~ *mom*	mom	*substitution*
who (did) got	who got	*omission, substitution*
people (from) all other *sc*	[1]people all other [2]people from all over	*self-correction*
me to go	me to go	
called me	call me	
right now	right nee	
didn't like it	didn't it like	
and a little	and a tiny	
her own room	[1]her and own room [2]her own her own room	
in a room with Mike	[1]in room with Mike [2]in a room with Mike	
tried to play	treed to play	
this is a game	this is all game	
is a bad place	is a big bad place	

Note: In the "Student's Response," the superscripts [1] and [2] indicate the first and second response by the child.

For additional practice, complete the following chart.

Text Word	Student's Response	Classification
with your toys	your own toys	
Freddy's mother	Freddy mom	
If only I	If I	
old clothes	old cloths	
had to sleep	have to slip	
Darin said	Says Darin	
The year ahead	This yarn is hard	
should always be	[1]should always be [2]should always be	
designed a temple	signed a temple	
trade was reopened	trade was opened	
wear a helmet	wore a hulmet	
with the people	with these people	
the land of Punt	the country of Punt	
false beard	fearse board	

QUANTITATIVE ANALYSIS OF
READING LEVELS ON AN IRI

A student's reading level is determined on an IRI using two scores—*word-recognition percent correct* and *comprehension percent correct*—which are then evaluated according to standard criteria.

To calculate the word-recognition percent correct, the teacher counts the number of word-recognition errors in the passage, subtracts these from the total number of words in the passage, and divides that number by the total number of words in the passage.

$$\frac{\text{total words in passage} - \text{errors}}{\text{total words in passage}} = \text{word-recognition percent correct}$$

To determine the comprehension percent correct, the teacher subtracts the errors from the total number of questions and divides that number by the total number of questions.

$$\frac{\text{total number of questions} - \text{errors}}{\text{total questions for passage}} = \text{comprehension percent correct}$$

Once the percent correct scores for word recognition and comprehension have been determined, the next step is to evaluate the student's scores based on a set of criteria. There are several criteria from which to select, and while controversy persists over which criteria to use, any criteria is to be regarded only as an indicator or guide—not as a certainty. Two popular criteria that may be applied to IRI scores are those of Betts and Powell.

The most important function of an IRI may be the qualitative examination of the *nature* of word-recognition errors and self-corrections; therefore, the reading teacher should keep the quantitative criteria in mind but allow for flexibility if the resulting placement seems inappropriate.

The Betts Criteria

The following chart presents the *Betts criteria* (Betts, 1946) for characterizing three levels of reading difficulty by word-recognition skill and comprehension skill. Descriptively the student's reading behavior at the independent level is free from mispronunciations and comprehension errors. The reading is fluent and expressive. At the instructional, or "teaching," level, the student requires guidance or assistance. The student may read fluently but more slowly than at the independent level. At the frustration level, the student demonstrates considerable word-pronunciation difficulties and comprehension is impeded. Reading may become halting, the reader may become tense, and there may be observable behaviors of frustration, such as hair twisting, hair pulling, or facial grimacing.

Reading Level	Word-Recognition Percent Correct	Comprehension Percent Correct
Independent	99% and above	90% and above
Instructional	95–98%	75–89%
Frustration	90% and below	50% and below

To use the Betts criteria, the teacher compares the percent correct scores to those in the chart. For example, Brian, a third-grader, scored 100 percent on word recognition and comprehension on the third-grade passage. Then on the fourth-grade passage, which had 215 total words and 8 comprehension questions, he had 12 word-recognition errors and 6 comprehension errors. According to the formulae, Brian had 94 percent correct in word recognition and 25 percent correct in comprehension.

$$\frac{215 - 12}{215} = 94\% \qquad\qquad \frac{8 - 6}{8} = 25\%$$

When Brian's performance is compared to the chart, he is close to the instructional reading level in word recognition on the fourth-grade passage but definitely at a frustration reading level in comprehension. Based on these results, Brian should be placed in a high third-grade reader.

The Powell Criteria

To use the *Powell criteria* (Powell, 1968), the teacher applies the same formulae for word-recognition and comprehension percent correct as when using the Betts criteria. Powell established a differentiated criteria according to the level of the passage as shown in the chart below. The teacher locates in the left column of the chart the grade level of the passage administered to the child. Next, the teacher compares the student's word-recognition and comprehension percent correct scores with those to the right of the passage level. This determines the child's reading level.

Passage Grade Level	Word-Recognition Percent Correct	Comprehension Percent Correct	Reading Level
2nd and below	94% and above 87–93% below 87%	81% and above 55–80% below 55%	Independent Instructional Frustration
3rd to 5th	96% or greater 92–95% below 92%	85% and above 60–85% below 60%	Independent Instructional Frustration
6th and above	97% or greater 94–96% below 94%	91% and above 65–90% below 65%	Independent Instructional Frustration

Here is an example of one child's percent correct scores on three different reading passages:

Student	Passage Grade Level	Word-Recognition Percent Correct	Comprehension Percent Correct
Jimmy	2	95%	90%
	3	94%	80%
	4	90%	70%

Using the Powell criteria, we can see that Jimmy is at an independent reading level in both word recognition and comprehension on grade 2 material. On grade 3 material, Jimmy is at an instructional level. However, on grade 4 material, we note that Jimmy's comprehension is still at an instructional level, although his word recognition is at a frustration level. Because comprehension is more important to classroom learning than word recognition, Jimmy's placement is more heavily influenced by his comprehension score. Jimmy can be initially placed in grade 3 reading materials for instruction and given more difficult material if he is successful. Jimmy should be provided grade 2 materials for his pleasure reading.

Here's another example:

Student	Passage Grade Level	Word-Recognition Percent Correct	Comprehension Percent Correct
Jane	2	90%	50%
	3	85%	50%

Jane's word recognition on grade 2 material is at the instructional level. However, her comprehension is at the frustration level. She is completely frustrated in both word recognition and comprehension at the grade 3 level. To determine her independent level and her instructional comprehension level, lower-grade level passages should be administered. Based on the information in the chart, Jane should probably be placed initially in grade 1 materials for instruction unless she shows signs of frustration and/or no progress, in which case a lower level of materials would be indicated.

ACTIVITY

DETERMINING READING LEVELS ON AN IRI

The purpose of this activity is to provide practice in determining independent, instructional, and frustration reading levels.

Directions: Using the data in the chart, calculate the word-recognition and comprehension percents correct, and determine the reading levels of each student based on one of the criteria. In this exercise, you are provided with the number of errors and, in parentheses, the total number of words in the passage and number of questions that followed. Thus, if on the chart a child has 10 (79) reported in word recognition, it means that out of 79 words in the passage, the child read 69 words correctly (10 errors). Divide the number correct (69) by the total (79) to determine the percent correct (87 percent).

Student	Passage Grade Level	Word-Recognition Errors	Word-Recognition Percent Correct	Compre-hension Errors	Compre-hension Percent Correct	Reading Level
Bernie	3	8 (138)[1]		1 (8)[2]		
	4	15 (162)		4 (8)		
Helen	1	2 (79)		1 (6)		
	2	5 (113)		2 (6)		
	3	11(119)		4 (8)		
Jackie	Primer	6 (50)		3 (6)		
	1	10 (79)		3 (6)		
	2	12 (113)		4 (6)		
Todd	5	12 (192)		1 (8)		
	6	10 (189)		1 (8)		
	7	11 (241)		2 (8)		

[1]Number of words in the reading passage.

[2]Number of comprehension questions asked on that passage.

A C T I V I T Y

DETERMINING READING LEVELS AND CALCULATING THE DEGREE OF A READING PROBLEM

The purpose of this activity is to provide practice in determining reading levels on an IRI and calculating the degree of a reading problem, using information from Chapters 5 and 6.

Part 1: Using Criteria to Determine Reading Levels

Directions: Using the data in the chart, calculate the word-recognition and comprehension percent correct, and determine the reading levels of each student based on the criteria specified by your instructor. In this exercise, you are provided with the number of errors and, in parentheses, the total number of words in the passage or questions that followed. Thus, if on the chart a child has 5 (85) reported in word recognition, it means that out of 85 words in the passage, the child read 80 words correctly (5 errors). Divide the number correct (80) by the total (85) to determine the percent correct (95 percent).

Student	Passage Grade Level	Word-Recognition Errors	Word-Recognition Percent Correct	Compre-hension Errors	Compre-hension Percent Correct	Reading Level
Andrea	2	6 (119)[1]		2 (8)[2]		
	3	10 (162)		5 (8)		
	4	17 (215)		7 (8)		
Derek	Primer	6 (50)		1 (6)		
	1	13 (79)		2 (6)		
Elizabeth	Primer	0 (50)		0 (6)		
	1	8 (79)		2 (6)		
	2	13 (113)		1 (6)		
	3	19 (138)		6 (8)		

[1]Number of words in the reading passage.

[2]Number of comprehension questions asked on that passage.

Part 2: Calculating the Degree of a Reading Problem

Directions: Given the information below and the IRI reading levels determined from Part 1, calculate the degree of the reading problem for each child using *either* the Harris reading expectancy age formula and the degree of tolerable difference *or* the reading expectancy and reading quotient formulae. For each child, explain whether there is a reading problem, the degree of the problem, and what led you to that conclusion.

1. Andrea was tested in the summer before she entered fifth grade. Her IQ is approximately 105, and her chronological age is 9 years 11 months.

2. Derek was tested in January of his second-grade year. His IQ is approximately 103, and his chronological age is 9 years 11 months. He had repeated kindergarten.

3. Elizabeth was tested in August before she entered third grade. Her listening comprehension level is estimated at fourth grade. Her chronological age is 8 years 11 months.

QUALITATIVE ANALYSIS OF ORAL READING ERRORS

As previously stated, perhaps the most important function of the IRI is the interpretation of oral reading and comprehension errors. The teacher examines oral reading errors to determine which ones interfere most with comprehension and to look for patterns of behavior that may provide insight into the strategies the student is using. Examining a student's responses to comprehension questions may also provide clues to the student's reading strategies. For instance, the teacher may observe that the student uses background knowledge and context clues to gain meaning but has poor word recognition strategies.

Once testing is completed, the teacher summarizes the student's oral reading errors as a first step in finding such patterns. An *Oral Reading Behavior Analysis Form* and *Summary Sheet* are provided for this purpose.

Oral Reading Behavior Analysis Form

The teacher completes one analysis form for each passage the student reads orally and uses this form to analyze substitutions and mispronunciations. Each form has spaces for the student's name, the date of testing, and the passage grade level. Next, the form has a chart with the following headings: Text Word, Student's Response, Semantic Appropriateness, Syntactic Appropriateness, **Graphic Similarity**, and Comments.

In the column labeled "Text Word," the teacher writes the word from the text in which the error occurred. In the "Student's Response" column, the teacher writes what the child said. For example, if the text word was *little* and the child substituted *tiny*, the teacher would write *tiny* in this column. If the child mispronounced the text word, the teacher would write the child's response phonetically. For example, if the child said *lutle* for *little*, the teacher would write *lutle* in the second column.

The teacher then analyzes each response for its *semantic*, or meaning, appropriateness (column 3); *syntactic*, or grammatical, appropriateness (column 4); and *graphic similarity* of beginning, middle, and ending letters (column 5). Semantic and syntactic appropriateness are judged in the context of the sentence in which the error occurred. Look at each substitution/mispronunciation in a sentence and ask, "Does this make sense compared to the actual text?" and "Is this grammatically correct?" Comments (column 6) would include such things as finger pointing, head moving, squinting, and other behaviors that might indicate frustration or more specific information on the graphic, syntactic, or semantic error.

Below the chart for analyzing oral reading errors, the form lists five additional factors of reading behavior for the teacher to determine or report. Taken together, all the information will assist the teacher in making tentative instructional decisions. To ascertain some of this information, each IRI passage will need to be reexamined.

The first factor is *word accuracy rate*. This term is synonymous with word-recognition percent correct used in the quantitative analysis of reading level. The word accuracy rate is computed in the same way and should be noted in the appropriate space.

The second factor, the *self-correction rate*, is the number of self-corrections in the total error count. The total error count includes self-corrections; therefore, all initial errors are counted in the total errors. If the child made fifteen initial errors and self-corrected five of those, the rate is 5 of 15. Dividing 5 by 15 gives a self-correction rate of 33 percent.

The third factor on the form is *words aided* or *prompted*. The teacher simply writes the text words that were provided to the child during administration of the IRI.

The fourth factor, *comprehension accuracy rate*, is the same as comprehension percent correct used in determining reading level. That score is recorded in the space provided.

The fifth aspect, *solving strategies used*, requires careful thought. Once the other parts of the Oral Reading Behavior Analysis Form are completed, the teacher needs to reflect holistically on all of the child's reading behaviors and determine what strategies the child uses in his or her reading. Specific questions to guide this deliberation follow.

Questions to Determine Solving Strategies

I. **Behavior (Word Recognition)** SolvingStrategies/Needs

   1. The child makes excessive substitutions.

      a. Does the substitution make sense in the story/sentence? Reader uses context/linguistic clues.

         - Is the substitution a synonym for the text word?

         - Is the substitution in keeping with the context?

      b. Is the substitution grammatically and/or syntactically correct? Reader uses linguistic clues.

         - Is the substitution the same part of speech (noun for noun, etc.)?

         - Does the substitution agree with the text word in number and tense?

      c. Is the substitution graphically or phonemically similar to the text word? Reader uses visual and phonic clues.

         - Does the substitution/mispronunciation contain the same first letter as the text word? First and last letters?

         - Does the substitution/mispronunciation contain the same vowel sound as the text word?

         - Does the child break up unknown words into sound units?

   2. The child makes many repetitions.

      Does the child reread the text when an error causes a meaning discrepancy? Reader uses context and/or language clues.

         - Are repetitions used to self-correct?

         - Are repetitions used to aid in word recognition?

   3. The child makes many additions and omissions in oral reading.

      Is comprehension intact with the additions and omissions? Reader uses context but may have too large an eye-voice span.

   4. The child misreads the simplest words.

      Does the reader mispronounce, or refuse to pronounce, frequently used words? Reader has a poor sight vocabulary.

   5. The child frustrates at a pre-primer level.

      a. Does the reader know any words on the basic sight word list? Reader has poor sight vocabulary.

      b. Does the child confuse letters or fail to identify letters of the alphabet? Reader may lack visual discrimination skills.

II. **Behavior (Comprehension)**	**SolvingStrategies/Needs**
6. Does child read word by word rather than in phrases?	Reader focuses on visual and phonic clues.
7. Is child's silent reading comprehension higher than oral reading comprehension?	Reader focuses on correct pronunciation instead of gaining meaning.
8. Are comprehension errors mainly at the inferential or evaluation levels?	Reader reads for details.
9. Does child have difficulty with word meanings? Did lack of vocabulary knowledge cause a comprehension question to be missed?	Reader lacks appropriate vocabulary/oral language skills.
10. Did the child answer a question correctly in spite of key mispronunciations? Did the child answer a question correctly with information outside the passage?	Reader has good background, or schema.

Summary Sheet

After completing an Oral Reading Behavior Analysis Form for each passage read and answering some of the questions to determine the student's solving strategies and needs, the teacher then fills out the Summary Sheet. The Summary Sheet allows for compilation of all data from the IRI testing and also includes a section for instructional recommendations.

For future reference, the teacher gathers the test forms on which the oral reading errors and comprehension responses are recorded, along with the Oral Reading Behavior Analysis Form and Summary Sheet. These forms are placed in a child's individual folder. Observation data, samples of the student's work, and additional information from tests or diagnostic lessons should be kept in this folder to assist in lesson planning, parent-teacher conferences, and referrals.

SAMPLE
IRI (Mary)

The following pages contain examples of marked IRI passages for a student named Mary, completed Oral Reading Behavior Analysis Forms for each passage, as well as a completed Summary Sheet. Mary's quantitative errors were analyzed using the Powell criteria. An interpretation of Mary's reading behavior follows the passages.

Passage Grade Level 3

Air Travel

Air travel is the newest and fastest way to carry people. Air traffic grows each year.

Airplanes can go a long way in a short time. People in a jet ride in comfort. They can eat meals on the plane. They can listen to music. They can *see* ~~watch~~ a movie. Airplanes come in many sizes. Some airplanes can only fit two people. Others can carry 300 people.

Some airplanes move only cargo. Cargo can be boxes, machines, or food. Most mail is sent by airplane. Airplanes are very important to our way of life.

All the large cities in the United States can be reached by air. In fact, we can go to any country by air. Travel has been made easier because of airplanes.

Flying planes need help so they don't crash into each other. Control towers are found in every airport. The *towers* ~~tower~~ is usually at the top of a tall building. The tower has glass walls all around it. The people who work in the tower help the pilots. They watch radar screens to be sure the airplanes don't crash. They tell the pilots where to fly and land. They also tell them when to take off. These people help pilots when the plane is in trouble. Many people work in airports to help the pilots.   216 words

Substitutions	_2_	Repetitions	_0_
Additions	_0_	Reversals	_0_
Omissions	_0_	Self-corrections	_0_
Words Aided	_0_		

Comprehension Questions

+ 1. According to this story, what are some things people can do in a plane? (eat meals; listen to music; watch a movie)

   eat, watch movies

+ 2. Where is a control tower? (at the top of a tall building; in an airport)

   in an airport

+ 3. What is said that makes you think air travel is safe? (People watch radar screens; people help pilots.)

   radar screens
   People talk to the pilot.

+ 4. Why do you think the control tower has glass walls? (so people can watch the planes in the air and in the airport)

   so people can see the planes

+ 5. How is a pilot like the driver of a car? (They steer the car or plane.)

   He drives the airplane.

+ 6. What is another title for this story? (Flying; Going by Air)

   Planes in the Air

+ 7. Why has travel been made easier because of airplanes? (We can go farther and faster.)

   We can go lots of places that are far away.

+ 8. What does the phrase *move cargo* mean? (carry boxes or freight)

   like carry stuff

ORAL READING BEHAVIOR ANALYSIS FORM

Student _Mary_ _____ Date of Testing _8/16/93_ _____

Passage Grade Level ___3_____

Text Word	Student's Response	Semantic Appropriateness	Syntactic Appropriateness	Graphic Similarity	Comments
watch	see	✓	✓	no	
tower	towers	✓	no	yes	

(continue on back if needed)   Reading Level:_✓_ Ind. _____ Inst. _____Frus.

Word Accuracy Rate (number words correct/total words in passage) = _214_ / _216_ = _99 %_

Self-correction (SC) Rate (number self-corrections/total errors) = _0_

Words Aided or Prompted (words given by examiner): _0_

Comprehension Accuracy Rate (number correct/total questions) = _100 %_

Solving Strategies Used (See Questions to Determine Solving Strategies):

Passage Grade Level 4

Pirates

Pirates sailed the seas many years ago. Pirates hunted and stole treasures on land and on the seas.

Men became pirates to get rich. As sailors, men were paid low ~~wages~~ *wagons* and conditions were usually poor on a ship. Piracy offered men a chance to get rich quickly. As pirates, they shared in "the loot."

Millions of dollars of riches ~~were~~ *was* stolen by pirates. They would capture gold, silver, jewelry, and money. Then they would divide it and take it back to their homes.

There was a lot of trouble on pirate ships. The men would fight among themselves and were usually not happy for very long. In fact, captains didn't last long. When men got angry or unhappy, they would elect a new captain. The old one was thrown overboard or killed. Two ~~famed~~ *famous* captains were Captain Kidd and Blackbeard.

Every crew had articles, or rules, written down. The rules set out the way pirates should act on (the) ship. The punishment was also spelled out in the articles. But no one has found any record yet of someone "walking the plank."

No one has ever found a real map of ~~buried~~ *burned* (sc) pirate treasure, either. Some ships that sunk in the ocean are thought to have treasure still on them. But the map with the big "X" is just a myth.   223 words

Substitutions	_3_		Repetitions	_1_
Additions	_0_		Reversals	_0_
Omissions	_1_		Self-corrections	_1_
Words Aided	_0_			

Comprehension Questions

+ 1. Why did men become pirates? (to get rich)

    to get rich

+ 2. Name two famous captains. (Captains Kidd and Blackbeard—must give both)

    Kidd and Blackbeard

+ 3. What were the articles on a pirate ship? (the laws or rules)

    laws

− 4. How are the articles on a ship like rules in school? (They both tell how to act and give the punishment if you break the rules.)

    don't know

+ 5. After the pirates stole treasure, what did they do with it? (divide it; share it)

    shared it

+ 6. What would cause the pirates to become angry or unhappy with their captain? (Answers will vary; this is a hypothesizing question. Reasonable answers would include: They disagreed with the captain over treasures, captain was unfair, they were at sea too long, etc.)

    if the captain was mean to them or wouldn't share the treasure

+ 7. What is a myth? (a story; a legend)

    like a story

+ 8. Why do you think people invented the story of buried treasure maps and walking the plank? (Answers will vary.)

    to make it more exciting

ORAL READING BEHAVIOR ANALYSIS FORM

Student ___Mary_____ Date of Testing ___8/16/93_____

Passage Grade Level ___4_____

Text Word	Student's Response	Semantic Appropriateness	Syntactic Appropriateness	Graphic Similarity	Comments
wages	wagons	no	✓	✓	initial OK
were	was	✓	no	✓	initial OK
famed	famous	✓	✓	✓	initial OK

(continue on back if needed)   Reading Level:___✓___ Ind. _____ Inst. _____Frus.

Word Accuracy Rate (number words correct/total words in passage) = 219 / 223 = 98 %

Self-correction (SC) Rate (number self-corrections/total errors) = 20 %

Words Aided or Prompted (words given by examiner): 0

Comprehension Accuracy Rate (number correct/total questions) = 88 %

Solving Strategies Used (See Questions to Determine Solving Strategies): used graphic aids (visual) and meaning cues

Passage Grade Level 5

Air Pollution

In the 16th century, Queen Elizabeth often ~~refused~~ *refined*[1] to visit the city of
London. She said that the air was too ~~polluted~~ *dirty*(A). The ~~pollution~~ *dirt*(A) came from
smoke from burning coal fires. When ~~fuels~~ *fowls*[2] are burned, they emit smoke that
has ~~poisonous~~ *poison*[3] gases. Most pollution today is caused by the same thing.

About 85 percent of the air ~~pollutants~~ *pollution*[4] in the United States are found in
smoke. The main ~~producers~~ *products*[5] of dangerous gases are cars, *and* factories, and power
plants. (The) burning of trash and garbage also add pollutants ~~to~~ *in*[6] the air.

Some air pollutants (are) ~~blown~~ *blow*[7] away by the wind. When the wind is not
blowing, the smoke does not go away. ~~Smog~~ *Smōg*[8] results from a mix of fog and
smoke. Smog *Smōg*[9] usually happens in very large cities. It looks like a dirt(y) cloud.

The pollutants in smoke and smog *smōg*[10] (can) cause disease. Air pollution is
~~harmful~~ *harming*(sc) to the nose, ~~throat~~ *thraut*(sc), and lungs. It is a ~~threat~~ *treat*[11] to our health.

146 words

Substitutions	11	Repetitions	1
Additions	1	Reversals	0
Omissions	4	Self-corrections	2
Words Aided	3		

Comprehension Questions

− 1. What causes air pollution? (burning gases; poisonous gases)

smŏg

− 2. What is smog? (a mixture of smoke and fog)

when the wind doesn't blow

− 3. Why does smog occur? (The pollutants are not blown away by the wind and they mix with the fog.)

don't know

+ 4. Why does smog usually happen in large cities? (There's a lot of smoke from the factories and more cars in bigger cities.)

They have lots of cars.

+ 5. Why is air pollution harmful to our health? (We breathe poisonous air and it can harm our lungs, etc.)

It's bad for your health, your lungs and stuff.

− 6. What does *emit* mean? (give out; send out)

have

+ 7. How is pollution today the same as pollution in the 16th century? (They burned coal which gave off pollution and we burn coal, oil, gasoline, and other gases.)

because we burn things

+ 8. What is the main idea of this passage? (Air pollution is caused by the burning of fuels.)

Air pollution is bad for us.

ORAL READING BEHAVIOR ANALYSIS FORM

Student ___*Mary*___   Date of Testing ___*8/16/93*___

Passage Grade Level ___*5*___

Text Word	Student's Response	Semantic Appropriateness	Syntactic Appropriateness	Graphic Similarity	Comments
refused	refined	no	✓	✓	missed medial sound
fuels	fowls	no	✓	✓	missed medial sound
poisonous	poison	✓	no	✓	missed ending
pollutants	pollution	✓	✓	✓	ending
producers	products	✓	✓	✓	ending
blown	blow	✓	no	✓	ending
Smog	Smōg	?	?	✓	medial sound
dirty	dirt	✓	no	✓	ending
threat	treat	no	✓	✓	"thr"

(continue on back if needed)   Reading Level:_____ Ind. _____ Inst. ___✓_Frus.

Word Accuracy Rate (number words correct/total words in passage) = *130/146 = 89 %*

Self-correction (SC) Rate (number self-corrections/total errors) = *2/19 = 10 %*

Words Aided or Prompted (words given by examiner): *polluted   pollution   emit*

Comprehension Accuracy Rate (number correct/total questions) = *50 %*

Solving Strategies Used (See Questions to Determine Solving Strategies):

attends to graphic, particularly the initial sounds
Uses meaning clues

SUMMARY SHEET

Student __Mary__   Grade __4__   Sex __F__

Birthdate __2/18/83__   Chronological Age __10__

School __Fairfield Ele__   Teacher __Gonzalez__

Test Administered by __Gonzalez__   Date of Testing __8/16/93__

Independent Reading Level   __3.4__

Instructional Reading Level   __4__

Frustration Reading Level   __5__

Listening Level   __N.A.__

Reading Strengths

- uses meaning cues, visual cues (graphic),
- attends to initial phonic cues, comprehension skills

Reading Needs

- some medial sounds may need review
- few self-corrections (Is she monitoring as she reads?)

Instructional Recommendations

Review medial sounds, perhaps review syllabication, work with metacognitive strategies.
Increase silent reading opportunities and give a structured vocabulary program.

Interpretation

Mary read grade-level passages 3 through 5. On the grade 3 and grade 4 passages, she was independent in word recognition and comprehension. On the grade 5 passage, Mary clearly frustrated in both word recognition and comprehension. As there is no clear instructional passage, the grade 4 level is considered her instructional level.

Mary's strengths are that she uses several positive solving strategies. Almost all of her substitutions were graphically similar to the text word. Of Mary's 15 substitution errors, 10 were semantically correct and 5 were syntactically correct. Based on the solving strategies, Mary uses context and linguistic cues as well as phonic and visual cues.

There appears to be no problem with repetitions, additions, or omissions.

A C T I V I T Y

ANALYZING RESULTS OF AN IRI

In this exercise, you are presented with marked IRI passages. These are graded passages with accompanying comprehension questions that have been administered to a child.

You have had experience in determining reading levels and in classifying and marking reading behaviors. Now you will examine marked passages to determine the number of errors and percent of correct responses in word recognition and comprehension. From this quantitative data, you will be able to identify the reading levels of the child.

In addition, you will be required to analyze qualitatively the child's performance, using the Oral Reading Behavior Analysis Forms and Summary Sheet.

Directions: The following pages contain three IRI passages administered to one child. The child's oral reading behaviors have been marked and answers to the comprehension questions are included.

1. Record and analyze the child's oral reading errors and comprehension responses on the Oral Reading Behavior Analysis Forms and the Summary Sheet.
2. Determine the child's reading levels (independent, instructional, and frustration), and note them on the Summary Sheet.
3. Determine whether the child has a reading problem.

4. Determine the child's reading strengths and needs.
5. Specify at least three instructional decisions on the Summary Sheet under Instructional Recommendations.

Note: Based on a graded word list, passage administration for this child began with grade 3.

Information on child

Name: *Jane*   Birthdate: *4/25/82*   Sex: *F*

Grade Placement	*6.3 (at time of testing)*
School	*Taylor Middle School*
Predominant Reading Method	*basal*
Chronological Age	*11 years 5 months*
IQ range (68 percent confidence level)	*102–110*

Passage Grade Level 3

Air Travel

Air travel is the newest and fastest way to carry people. Air traffic grows each year.

Airplanes can go a long way in a short time. People in a jet ride in comfort. They can eat meals on the plane. They can listen to music. They can watch a movie. Airplanes come in many sizes. Some airplanes can only fit two people. Others can carry 300 people.

Some airplanes move only cargo. Cargo can be boxes, machines, or food. Most mail is sent by airplane. Airplanes are very important to our way of life.

All the large cities in the United States can be reached by air. In fact, we can go to any country by air. Travel has been made ~~easier~~ *easy* because of airplanes.

Flying planes need help so they don't crash into each other. Control towers are found in every airport. The tower is usually at the top of a tall building. The tower has glass walls all around. The people who work in the tower help the pilots. They watch radar screens to be sure the airplanes don't crash. They tell pilots where to fly and land. They also tell them when to take off. These people help pilots when the plane is in trouble. Many people work in airports to help the pilots.   216 words

Substitutions	_____	Repetitions	_____
Additions	_____	Reversals	_____
Omissions	_____	Self-corrections	_____
Words Aided	_____		

Comprehension Questions

1. According to this story, what are some things people can do in a plane? (eat meals; listen to music; watch a movie)

    eat

2. Where is a control tower? (at the top of a tall building; in an airport)

    at the airport

3. What is said that makes you think air travel is safe? (People watch radar screens; people help pilots.)

    They don't crash.

4. Why do you think the control tower has glass walls? (so people can watch the planes in the air and in the airport)

    to look out at the planes

5. How is a pilot like the driver of a car? (They steer the car or plane.)

    He drives it where he's going.

6. What is another title for this story? (Flying; Going by Air)

    Air Travel
    ? - Going on a Plane

7. Why has travel been made easier because of airplanes? (We can go farther and faster.)

    It's fast.

8. What does the phrase *move cargo* mean? (carry boxes or freight)

    when the men carry the boxes and things from the plane

ORAL READING BEHAVIOR ANALYSIS FORM

Student _____ Date of Testing _____

Passage Grade Level _____

Text Word	Student's Response	Semantic Appropriateness	Syntactic Appropriateness	Graphic Similarity	Comments

(continue on back if needed)   Reading Level:_____ Ind. _____ Inst. _____Frus.

Word Accuracy Rate (number words correct/total words in passage) =

Self-correction (SC) Rate (number self-corrections/total errors) =

Words Aided or Prompted (words given by examiner):

Comprehension Accuracy Rate (number correct/total questions) =

Solving Strategies Used (See Questions to Determine Solving Strategies):

Passage Grade Level 4

Pirates

Pirates sailed the seas many years ago. Pirates hunted and stole treasures [A] on land and on the seas.

Men became pirates to get rich. As sailors, men were paid low wages and conditions were ~~usually~~ *unusually* poor on a ship. Piracy offered men a chance to get rich quick(ly) As pirates, they shared in "the loot."

Millions of dollars of riches were stolen by pirates. They would capture gold, silver, ~~jewels~~ *jewelry*, and money. Then they would divide it and take it back (to their home(s.)

There was a lot of trouble on pirate ships. The men would fight among themselves and were usually not happy for very long. In fact, captains didn't last long. When the men got angry or unhappy, they would elect a new captain. The old one was thrown overboard or killed. Two famous captains were Captain Kidd and Blackbeard.

Every crew had ~~articles~~ *art* [A], or rules, written down. The rules set out the way pirates should act on the ship. The punishment was also spelled out in the [A] articles. But no one has found any record (yet) of someone "walking the ~~plank~~ *plant*."

No one has (ever) *even* found a real map of buried pirate treasure, either. Some ships that ~~sunk~~ *sink* in the ocean are thought to have treasure still on them. But the map with the big "X" is just a ~~myth~~ *mithe*.   223 words

Substitutions	_____	Repetitions	_____
Additions	_____	Reversals	_____
Omissions	_____	Self-corrections	_____
Words Aided	_____		

Comprehension Questions

1. Why did men become pirates? (to get rich)

    to get rich

2. Name two famous captains. (Captains Kidd and Blackbeard—must give both)

    Kidd and Blackbeard

3. What were the articles on a pirate ship? (the laws or rules)

    rules

4. How are the articles on a ship like rules in school? (They both tell how to act and give the punishment if you break the rules.)

    They tell people how to act.

5. After the pirates stole treasure, what did they do with it? (divide it; share it)

    took it home

6. What would cause the pirates to become angry or unhappy with their captain? (Answers will vary; this is a hypothesizing question. Reasonable answers would include: They disagreed with the captain over treasures, captain was unfair, they were at sea too long, etc.)

    lots of things
    ? - maybe he kept the money or he killed their friend

7. What is a myth? (a story; a legend)

    don't know

8. Why do you think people invented the story of buried treasure maps and walking the plank? (Answers will vary.)

    so people would read it

ORAL READING BEHAVIOR ANALYSIS FORM

Student _____ Date of Testing _____

Passage Grade Level _____

Text Word	Student's Response	Semantic Appropriateness	Syntactic Appropriateness	Graphic Similarity	Comments

(continue on back if needed)   Reading Level:_____ Ind. _____ Inst. _____Frus.

Word Accuracy Rate (number words correct/total words in passage) =

Self-correction (SC) Rate (number self-corrections/total errors) =

Words Aided or Prompted (words given by examiner):

Comprehension Accuracy Rate (number correct/total questions) =

Solving Strategies Used (See Questions to Determine Solving Strategies):

Passage Grade Level 5

Air Pollution

In the 16th century, Queen Elizabeth (often) ~~refused~~ *re' fused* to visit the city of

London. She said that the air was too polluted. The pollution came from

smoke from burning coal fires. When ~~fuels~~ *fires* are burned, they emit *A* smoke that

has ~~poisonous~~ *poison* gases. Most pollution today is caused by the same thing.

←About 85 percent of the air pollutants in the ~~United States~~ *U. S.* are found in

smoke. The main ~~producers~~ *pollutions* of dangerous gases are cars, factories, and power

plants. The burning of trash and garbage *garbage SC* also add ~~pollutants~~ *pollution* to the air.

Some air pollutants are blown (away) by the wind. When the wind ~~is not~~ *isn't*

blowing, the smoke does not go away. Smog results from a mix of fog and

smoke. Smog usually *unusual SC* happens in very large cities. It looks like a dirty cloud.

The pollutants in smoke and smog (can) cause disease. Air pollution is

harmful to the nose, ~~throat~~ *treat*, and lungs. It is ~~a threat~~ *harmful* to our health.

146 words

Substitutions	_____		Repetitions	_____
Additions	_____		Reversals	_____
Omissions	_____		Self-corrections	_____
Words Aided	_____			

Comprehension Questions

1. What causes air pollution? (burning gases; poisonous gases)

    cars, factories

2. What is smog? (a mixture of smoke and fog)

    dirty cloud

3. Why does smog occur? (The pollutants are not blown away by the wind and they mix with the fog.)

    The wind stops blowing.

4. Why does smog usually happen in large cities? (There's a lot of smoke from the factories and more cars in bigger cities.)

    There's a lot of cars and people.

5. Why is air pollution harmful to our health? (We breathe poisonous air and it can harm our lungs, etc.)

    We get sick.

6. What does *emit* mean? (give out; send out)

    don't know

7. How is pollution today the same as pollution in the 16th century? (They burned coal which gave off pollution and we burn coal, oil, gasoline, and other gases.)

    don't know

8. What is the main idea of this passage? (Air pollution is caused by the burning of fuels.)

    Air pollution is harmful to our health.

ORAL READING BEHAVIOR ANALYSIS FORM

Student _____ Date of Testing _____

Passage Grade Level _____

Text Word	Student's Response	Semantic Appropriateness	Syntactic Appropriateness	Graphic Similarity	Comments

(continue on back if needed)   Reading Level:_____ Ind. _____ Inst. _____Frus.

Word Accuracy Rate (number words correct/total words in passage) =

Self-correction (SC) Rate (number self-corrections/total errors) =

Words Aided or Prompted (words given by examiner):

Comprehension Accuracy Rate (number correct/total questions) =

Solving Strategies Used (See Questions to Determine Solving Strategies):

SUMMARY SHEET

Student _____ Grade _____ Sex _____

Birthdate _____ Chronological Age _____

School _____ Teacher _____

Test Administered by _____ Date of Testing _____

Independent Reading Level   _____

Instructional Reading Level   _____

Frustration Reading Level   _____

Listening Level   _____

Reading Strengths

Reading Needs

Instructional Recommendations

ACTIVITY

ANALYZING RESULTS OF AN IRI

Directions: The following pages contain three IRI passages administered to one child. The child's oral reading behaviors have been marked, and answers to the comprehension questions are included. Analyze the results of this IRI following the directions on p. 95.

Note: Based on a graded word list, passage administration for this child began with grade 1.

Information on the child:

Name: *Al*   Birthdate: *9/28/84*   Sex: *M*

Grade Placement	*3.4 (at time of testing)*
School	*Ft. Brooks Elementary*
Predominant Reading Method	*basal*
Chronological Age	*9 years 2 months (repeated first grade)*
IQ range (68 percent confidence level)	*98–106*

Passage Grade Level 1

Families

No two families are the same. Some have many children. Some are small and may have (only) one child.

Some children live with their mother and father. Others may have only a
mother. Others may live with an aunt. Some children may have ~~foster~~ *faster*
parents.

Families live in many places. Some live in the city. They may live on a
farm. A family could live on a boat or in a ~~house~~ *home*.

But all families like to have fun. They go on trips. They play games. They go out to eat. They watch TV.

Families work together too. They share good and bad times. They love each other.

Families are not the same and they are the same.   118 words

Substitutions	_____	Repetitions	_____
Additions	_____	Reversals	_____
Omissions	_____	Self-corrections	_____
Words Aided	_____		

Comprehension Questions

1. How are families different? (They live in different places; they have different members.)

   Some are big and some are small.

2. Where are some places that families live? (houses, the city, boats, farms)

   farm, city

3. How are families the same? (They like to have fun; they work together, etc.)

   They love each other.

4. What would be another title for this story? (Family Life; Different Families)

   What's a Family?

5. What does the sentence *Families are not the same and they are the same* mean? (Families may be different in number or in where they live, but they are the same in that they have fun together.)

   some are the same

   ? - no response

6. How do families work together? (They work in the yard or around the house; they work on special things; they help each other.)

   They help each other doing chores.

ORAL READING BEHAVIOR ANALYSIS FORM

Student _____ Date of Testing _____

Passage Grade Level _____

Text Word	Student's Response	Semantic Appropriateness	Syntactic Appropriateness	Graphic Similarity	Comments

(continue on back if needed)   Reading Level:_____ Ind. _____ Inst. _____ Frus.

Word Accuracy Rate (number words correct/total words in passage) =

Self-correction (SC) Rate (number self-corrections/total errors) =

Words Aided or Prompted (words given by examiner):

Comprehension Accuracy Rate (number correct/total questions) =

Solving Strategies Used (See Questions to Determine Solving Strategies):

Passage Grade Level 2

The Gold Rush

In 1840 San Francisco was a ~~tiny~~ *(A) teeny* town. One morning gold was found *(A)*

nearby. Soon everyone knew about the gold. People from all over came

looking for gold. This was called "The Gold Rush."

The people who went looking for gold were called "gold ~~diggers~~ *digs*." Some

people never got to the gold ~~fields~~ *fills*. There were no roads to mark the way.

Some died. Others became sick and turned back.

Most people lived in a mining town. *(A)* They lived in tents or ~~cabins~~ *kābins*. There

were very few women. The life was not easy (there.)

These small mining towns became cities. Very few people were lucky

enough to find gold. So they started stores. Some who did not find gold

became farmers. The people made laws and picked their leaders. Finding

gold in the West was important to the United States. *(A)*   138 words

Substitutions	_____	Repetitions	_____
Additions	_____	Reversals	_____
Omissions	_____	Self-corrections	_____
Words Aided	_____		

Comprehension Questions

1. Why was this time called "The Gold Rush"? (People went looking for gold after it was found.)

    don't know

2. What was said that makes you think it was difficult to go West looking for gold? (There were no roads; people got sick; people died, etc.)

    People died.

3. What were the people called who went looking for gold? (gold diggers)

    gold digs

4. What happened to those who didn't find gold? (Some became farmers or storekeepers.)

    They died.
    ? Some became farmers.

5. How is a cabin like a house? How are they different? (People live in them; they have similar shapes, etc.; a cabin can be smaller, more rustic, etc.)

    You live in it.

6. Why did people go searching for gold? (to get rich)

    to get rich

7. What would be another good title for this story? (Gold Diggers; Searching for Gold)

    Gold Digs

8. If gold were found in a town nearby, do you think there would be another gold rush? Why, or why not? (Answers will vary.)

    Yes, so they have lots of money.

ORAL READING BEHAVIOR ANALYSIS FORM

Student _____ Date of Testing _____

Passage Grade Level _____

Text Word	Student's Response	Semantic Appropriateness	Syntactic Appropriateness	Graphic Similarity	Comments

(continue on back if needed)   Reading Level:_____ Ind. _____ Inst. _____Frus.

Word Accuracy Rate (number words correct/total words in passage) =

Self-correction (SC) Rate (number self-corrections/total errors) =

Words Aided or Prompted (words given by examiner):

Comprehension Accuracy Rate (number correct/total questions) =

Solving Strategies Used (See Questions to Determine Solving Strategies):

Passage Grade Level 3

Air Travel

Air travel is ~~the~~ _new_ ~~newest~~ and ~~fastest~~ _fast_ way to carry people. Air traffic grows [A]

each year.

Airplanes can go a long way in a short time. People in a jet ride in

comfort. [A] They can eat (meals) on the plane. They can ~~listen~~ _hear_ to music. They can

watch a movie. Airplanes come in many sizes. Some airplanes can only fit

two people. Others can carry 300 people.

Some airplanes move only ~~cargo~~ _cars_. ~~Cargo~~ _cars_ can be boxes, machines, or food.

Most mail is sent by airplane. Airplanes are very important to our way of life.

All the large cities in the United States can be reached [A] by air. In fact, we

can go to any country by air. Travel has been made ~~easier~~ _easy_ because of

airplanes.

Flying planes need help so they don't crash (into each other). Control [A]

~~towers~~ _tools_ are found in every airport. The ~~tower~~ _trol_ is (usually) at the top of a tall

building. The ~~tower~~ _trol_ has glass walls all around. The people who work in the

~~tower~~ _trol_ help the pilots. They watch radar [A] screens [A] to be sure the airplanes don't

crash. They tell the pilots ~~where~~ _when_ to fly and land. They also tell them when to

take off. These people help pilots when the plane is in trouble. Many people

work in airports to help the pilots.   216 words

Substitutions	_____	Repetitions	_____
Additions	_____	Reversals	_____
Omissions	_____	Self-corrections	_____
Words Aided	_____		

Comprehension Questions

1. According to this story, what are some things people can do in a plane? (eat meals; listen to music; watch a movie)

   eat, read

2. Where is a control tower? (at the top of a tall building; in an airport)

   don't know

3. What is said that makes you think air travel is safe? (People watch radar screens; people help pilots.)

   Planes don't crash into each other.

4. Why do you think the control tower has glass walls? (so people can watch the planes in the air and in the airport)

   to see outside

5. How is a pilot like the driver of a car? (They steer the car or plane.)

   They both make it go.

6. What is another title for this story? (Flying; Going by Air)

   Flying

7. Why has travel been made easier because of airplanes? (We can go farther and faster.)

   We can go places.

8. What does the phrase *move cargo* mean? (carry boxes or freight)

   move things

ORAL READING BEHAVIOR ANALYSIS FORM

Student _____ Date of Testing _____

Passage Grade Level _____

Text Word	Student's Response	Semantic Appropriateness	Syntactic Appropriateness	Graphic Similarity	Comments

(continue on back if needed)   Reading Level:_____ Ind. _____ Inst. _____Frus.

Word Accuracy Rate (number words correct/total words in passage) =

Self-correction (SC) Rate (number self-corrections/total errors) =

Words Aided or Prompted (words given by examiner):

Comprehension Accuracy Rate (number correct/total questions) =

Solving Strategies Used (See Questions to Determine Solving Strategies):

SUMMARY SHEET

Student _____ Grade _____ Sex _____

Birthdate _____ Chronological Age _____

School _____ Teacher _____

Test Administered by _____ Date of Testing _____

Independent Reading Level   _____

Instructional Reading Level   _____

Frustration Reading Level   _____

Listening Level   _____

Reading Strengths

Reading Needs

Instructional Recommendations

A C T I V I T Y

ADMINISTERING AND INTERPRETING AN IRI

Directions: Administer a published IRI to a child. Determine the child's reading levels, reading strengths, and reading needs, and make two to five instructional recommendations. A blank Oral Reading Analysis Form and Summary Sheet are provided in Appendix C for you to use in this activity.

SUMMARY

A diagnostic method for gathering information on a student's reading levels and solving strategies is the informal reading inventory. In this chapter, you had experiences with marking an IRI as well as interpreting a student's responses. You will find the information gained from an IRI invaluable in instructional decision making.

SUGGESTED READINGS

Farr, R., & Carey, R. F. (1986). *Reading: What can be measured?* (2nd ed.). Newark, DE: International Reading Association.

Gillet, J., & Temple, C. (1990). *Understanding reading problems* (3rd ed.). Glenview, IL: Scott, Foresman/Little, Brown.

Leslie, L., & Caldwell, J. (1990). *Qualitative reading inventory.* Glenview, IL: Scott, Foresman/Little, Brown.

Richek, M. A., List, Lynne K., & Lerner, J. W. (1989). *Reading problems: Assessment and teaching strategies* (2nd ed.). Englewood Cliffs, NJ: Prentice Hall.

Woods, M. L., & Moe, A. J. (1988). *Analytical reading inventory* (4th ed.). Columbus, OH: Charles C. Merrill.

CHAPTER 7 / EVALUATING COMPREHENSION STRATEGIES

There are some aspects of comprehension that cannot be evaluated through the use of standardized tests or informal reading inventories. Standardized tests and informal reading inventories provide only gross estimates of a student's ability to handle the textbooks utilized in the classroom. If a teacher wants to evaluate a student's knowledge of text structure, background knowledge, knowledge of language, prediction abilities, and content reading ability, different assessment strategies are needed.

Alexander and Heathington (1988) state that process measures attempt to "understand and measure comprehension as it is occurring." Thus, the teacher needs a more interactive approach in measuring comprehension strategies. The informal reading inventory with qualitative error analysis, examined in Chapter 6, is one type of process measure. The cloze test, with an applied error analysis, is another. This chapter discusses the cloze test, the content reading inventory, and the group reading inventory, which incorporate techniques to evaluate some of the comprehension processes.

This chapter provides a variety of teaching techniques useful for comprehension evaluation. Some of these alternative assessment techniques attempt to measure students' metacognitive comprehension processes, such as predicting strategies, self-questioning, and summarizing. Most of these assessment strategies can be used both individually and in a written form that allows for small-group evaluation.

THE CLOZE TEST

The *cloze test* is an informal technique used to determine (1) the readability of written material; (2) an individual's reading level on specific material; (3) an individual's vocabulary level in a specific subject or topic area; (4) an individual's language skills; and (5) an estimate of an individual's general comprehension level. Cloze can also provide a reading level profile of a class or small group.

Cloze uses student materials—that is, materials used in the classroom, such as content textbooks, workbooks, or other required reading. With a standard cloze, the selected passage is duplicated and words at regularly spaced intervals are omitted from the passage. These omitted words are called *cloze units*. The reader's task is to supply the cloze units from the remaining context. The appropriateness of the material for each student depends on the percentage of correct answers. Criteria have been developed to help the teacher determine if the material used in the classroom will be suitable for the students.

Constructing the Cloze Test

To construct a standard cloze test, select a passage unfamiliar to the students that is approximately 250 to 300 words in length. The passage should come from the students' content textbooks or other required reading material. The first sentence is left intact. Beginning with the second sentence, count and delete every fifth word if the test is to be used in grades 4 and up. However, if a cloze is constructed for the primary grades, eliminate every seventh or tenth word. Proper nouns (Dan, Tampa, Lincoln, etc.) are skipped, and the next word is deleted. Words are eliminated until there are a total of 50 deletions. With primary students, you may need to have two passages of 25 deletions administered on different days for a total of 50 deletions. The last sentence is left intact. Deleted words are replaced with a blank line approximately fifteen typed spaces in length. For example:

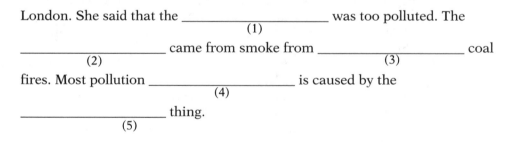

In the 16th century, Queen Elizabeth often refused to visit the city of

London. She said that the _____ was too polluted. The
                                    (1)

_____ came from smoke from _____ coal
           (2)   (3)

fires. Most pollution _____ is caused by the
                              (4)

_____ thing.
          (5)

Administering the Cloze Test

Before administering the test, provide the students with five to ten practice sentences so they can familiarize themselves with the procedure. Directions to the students should include the following:

1. They are to write only one word in the blank space, even though there may be many words that "fit" the meaning of the passage.
2. They are to pick the word that they feel best completes the sentence and "fits" the meaning of the passage.
3. They are not expected to get all the answers correct; if they do not know an answer on the first try, they should skip it and come back to it later.
4. They should first read the entire passage quickly, and then read it a second time to fill in the blanks.
5. There is no time limit to the test.

Scoring the Cloze Test

Only the *exact* replacement is scored as a correct response—that is, only the deleted word is acceptable, not a synonym or another form of the correct word. Although more than one word might easily make sense for a specific cloze unit, only the deleted word should be counted as an accurate response when using cloze to determine a student's reading level or the appropriateness of materials for students. Accepting synonyms or other forms for the required words drastically reduces the reliability of the cloze test. If the purpose of the cloze is instructional (for example, to practice use of context or to work on vocabulary development) synonyms and other forms of the extracted word are acceptable. Look at the following excerpt from a completed cloze test:

In the 16th century, Queen Elizabeth often refused to visit the city of

London. She said that the _____*city*_____ was too polluted. The
(1) air

_____*pollution*_____ came from smoke from _____*burned*_____ coal
(2) pollution   (3) burning

fires. Most pollution _____*everywhere*_____ is caused by the
(4) today

_____*same*_____ thing.
(5) same

This student had 2 exact replacements in the first 5 deletions. *City* makes sense and even fits the sense of the passage but cannot be counted as correct because it is not an exact replacement. *Burned,* although a form of the deleted word, cannot be counted as correct because the exact replacement is *burning.*

To determine the percent of correct responses, divide the number of correct responses by the total number of blanks. So, if a student correctly replaced twenty-five of the fifty possible cloze units, his or her score would be 50 percent.

Criteria for Evaluating Cloze Test Scores

While 50% may seem low, for cloze criteria it is an acceptable rate of correct response. There are several criteria for judging cloze scores; the most widely used was developed by Rankin and Culhane (1969). Their guidelines, presented below, relate to independent, instructional, and frustration reading levels.

Percent of Correct Responses	Reading Level
60% and above	Independent
40–59%	Instructional
below 40%	Frustration

When the cloze is given to an entire class or a group of students, the scores can be summarized on a chart (see page 132). Because the cloze was developed from classroom reading material, the teacher can readily see which students will be able to handle the text material independently, which will need guidance, and which will need considerable assistance.

Cloze Results September 14, 1993
Social Studies, Grade 6

Students with 60% and above correct	Students with 40–59% correct	Students with below 40% correct
Chimer Andrews Bill Yates	Andre White Missy Hite	Cathy Timmons Benita Adams

Analyzing Cloze Test Responses

When the cloze test is employed to examine the comprehension strategies of individual students, an *applied error analysis* is used much the same way as the error analysis in Chapter 6. Each response can be categorized to determine the possible strategies a child is using. One category system the teacher can utilize in the classroom was developed by Shearer (1982).

1. Count the number of exact replacements (ER), and determine the percent correct.

$$\frac{\text{exact replacements (ER)}}{\text{total deletions}} = \text{percent correct}$$

2. Examine the errors, and categorize them according to the following descriptions:

    a. Synonyms (SYN): Words that mean the same as the deleted word.

    b. Semantically Appropriate (SEM): Words that make sense in the sentence but not necessarily in the context of the passage. The word may not reflect the intended meaning of the author.

    c. Semantic/Not Syntactic (SEM/NStc): Words that indicate meaning but are not syntactically appropriate. May not be the same part of speech or agree in number or tense with the deleted word. For example:

    The boy _____*jump*_____ the fence.
    jumped

    d. Syntactically Appropriate (STC): Words that are the same part of speech as the deleted words and agree in number and tense, where appropriate, but are not semantically appropriate. For example:

    Most pollution _____*sometimes*_____ is caused
    today

    e. Nonsense Errors (NON): Nonwords or words that do not make sense in the sentence and are not syntactically appropriate.

    f. Omissions (OM): No response.

3. Determine the percent for each category of error:

$$\frac{\text{error category}}{\text{total errors}} = \text{percent of error category in total errors}$$

For example, a student has 15 exact replacements and 35 total errors. The percent correct is 30. The errors fell into the following categories:

Category	Number of Errors	Percentage
SYN	5	14%
SEM	10	28%
SEM/NStc	1	3%
STC	8	23%
NON	6	17%
OM	5	14%

Interpreting Cloze Test Responses

By looking at the percent of each type of error, the teacher determines that this student is using language cues during reading even though the passage is at a frustration reading level. The high percent of semantically and syntactically appropriate errors indicate the student is gaining meaning and reads contextually. It may also indicate the student has highly developed schemata for the content.

SCORING AND ANALYZING A CLOZE TEST

The purpose of this task is for you to score and analyze a cloze test.

Directions: The following cloze passage is on a grade 3 reading level and was given to an 11-year-old boy in the fifth grade with reading problems. The responses are spelled exactly as he wrote them on his answer sheet. Score the cloze to determine reading level and using the Cloze Test Applied Error Analysis Sheet, analyze the errors according to the method provided in the text. Then write a brief summary of the results.

Cloze Passage: Early Trains

Long before there were cars and airplanes, there were railroad trains.

The early trains were _____*build*_____ up of one or
(1) made

_____*more*_____ railroad cars. These cars _____*were*_____
(2) two   (3) were

pulled by a steam _____*engine*_____ . These steam engines were
(4) engine

_____*big*_____ "iron horses."
(5) called

Early trains _____ go faster and carry
(6) could

_____*some*_____ goods than any other _____ of
(7) more   (8) kind

transportation. Railroad tracks _____ put in many parts
(9) were

_____*of*_____ the United States. It _____*had*_____ many
(10) of   (11) took

men to lay _____*the*_____ tracks. The men had
(12) down

_____*to*_____ fight Indians and ranchers. _____*The Indians*_____
(13) to   (14) They

didn't want their land _____*to*_____ by trains.
(15) used

Along the _____*railroad*_____ new towns sprang up.
(16) tracks

_____*Some*_____ towns by the railroad _____*got*_____
(17) Old   (18) grew

bigger. In 1869 the _____*railroad*_____ from the East met
(19) tracks

_____*the*_____ tracks from the West. A _____*railroad*_____
(20) the   (21) cross-country

network was started then. _____*This*_____ meant that people could
(22) This

_____*go*_____ from one end to _____*the*_____ other by
(23) travel   (24) the

train.

A trip _____ *in* _____ a train in the 1870s
(25) on

_____ *was* _____ an adventure. People could _____ *fight* _____
(26) was   (27) see

buffalo from the train. _____ *The* _____ trains would stop so
(28) Some

_____ *men* _____ could shoot the animals.
(29) people

_____ *The* _____ Indians didn't like people
(30) The

_____ *killing* _____ their buffalo. The buffalo _____ *was* _____
(31) shooting   (32) were

their main food. The Indians _____ *had* _____ to stop the railroad
(33) tried

_____ tearing up the tracks. _____ *Indians* _____ would
(34) by   (35) They

also shoot at _____ *the* _____ trains.
(36) the

Sometimes train robbers _____ *stop* _____ stop the trains. They
(37) would

_____ *might* _____ take things of value _____ *from* _____ the
(38) would   (39) from

people. They also _____ *stole* _____ the money being carried
(40) took

_____ *on* _____ the train.
(41) by

It did *n't* _____ cost a lot of _____ *money* _____ to ride
(42) not   (43) money

a train _____ *back* _____ those days. It cost _____ *about* _____
(44) in   (45) only

two or three cents _____ *one* _____ mile. A 30-mile trip
(46) a

_____ *was* _____ about 60 cents.
(47) cost

Today one _____ *train* _____ can pull 200 railroad
(48) engine

_____ *boxes* _____.
(49) cars

Railroads still carry people. _____ *And* _____ they also carry oil,
(50) But

coal, lumber, cars, and machines. Fewer people use trains today since we

have cars and airplanes.

CLOZE TEST APPLIED ERROR ANALYSIS SHEET

Student _____

Passage Grade Level _____

Material from Which Passage Was Derived _____

Date Administered _____

1. Exact replacements _____

   Percent correct _____

   Reading Level: _____ Independent _____ Instructional _____ Frustration

2. Total Errors _____

3. Determine the percent for each category of error.

Category	Number of Errors	Percent
SYN	_____	_____
SEM	_____	_____
SEM/NStc	_____	_____
STC	_____	_____
NON	_____	_____
OM	_____	_____

Possible Strategies Used

Needs

ACTIVITY

CONSTRUCTING, ADMINISTERING, AND SCORING A CLOZE TEST

The purpose of this task is for you to practice constructing, administering, scoring, and interpreting a cloze test.

Directions: Develop a cloze test to administer to an individual or to a group. You should develop the cloze from reading material used by the students. After administering and scoring the cloze, use the Cloze Test Applied Error Analysis Sheet to analyze and interpret the student's responses. Write a summary of the results and attach both the analysis sheet and your summary to your cloze test. (A blank analysis sheet is provided in Appendix C.)

THE CONTENT READING INVENTORY

The _content reading inventory (CRI)_ is an informal assessment technique that provides information on students' knowledge of book parts, reference aids, vocabulary, and comprehension of text material. It is a silent, group-administered test that is easily constructed, given, and scored. Its value to the classroom teacher is that the student's reading ability is measured on the text used for class instruction. It is most appropriate for students in grade 4 or higher.

There are three major sections of the CRI: (1) use of book parts and study aids; (2) vocabulary knowledge; and (3) comprehension. The following is a representative outline of a CRI (Readence, Bean, & Baldwin, 1989):

I. Textbook Aids/Study Aids
   A. Using book parts (table of contents, index, glossary, graphic aids, chapter introduction/summary, appendices, etc.)
   B. Using references (card catalog, encyclopedia, atlas, etc.)

II. Vocabulary Knowledge
   A. Recall of word meanings
   B. Use of context for word meanings

III. Comprehension
   A. Literal meanings
   B. Inferential meanings
   C. Passage organization

A CRI can be any length; however, the suggested _maximum_ number of questions is between 20 and 25 in one inventory. The age and reading ability of the students should determine the length of the inventory. There should be a maximum of 8 to 10 questions in section I, 4 to 6 in section II, and 7 to 9 in section III.

To construct the inventory, the teacher picks a three- to four-page selection from the text the students will be using. It should be a passage that the students have not read previously.

To administer the inventory, the teacher should read the questions orally to the students before they begin to ensure that they understand the questions. Students are told that the test does not count as part of their grade and that the information from the test will be used by the teacher in planning instruction. The CRI can be introduced as a class assignment for the purpose of familiarizing students with the text and, thus, alleviate any test anxiety.

Depending on the length of the inventory, it can be given on one or over two different days. If the inventory is given over two days, section I is given first, with sections II and III administered on the following day. To score the CRI, determine the percent of correct responses by dividing the number of correct responses by the total number of items. Judge each student's ability to read the text on the following criteria (McWilliams & Rakes, 1979):

Percent Correct	Text Difficulty
86–100%	Too easy
64–85%	Adequate for instruction
below 63%	Too difficult

If the text is deemed too difficult for a large portion of the group, the teacher will need to stress vocabulary and background development before the lesson. In addition, the inventory may identify students who miss a majority of questions within one section, such as study aids. These students, then, may benefit from **direct instruction** in that area.

Example of a Content Reading Inventory (Grade 4)

I.   Textbook Aids/Study Aids

Directions: Using your textbook or your previous knowledge, answer each of the following questions on a separate sheet of paper.

A.   Using Book Parts
   1. Where would you look to find information on "communities"?
   2. What topics does the book cover? Where did you find the information?
   3. What does Chapter 6 cover?
   4. Use the glossary to write a definition of *goods*.

B.   Using References
   5. What library aids would help you in locating a book on our nation's capital, Washington, DC?
   6. If you were going to give an oral report in class about government, would an encyclopedia help you? Why, or why not?
   7. Imagine that you want to make a time line of the life of Abraham Lincoln. Where would you look *first* for help?

II. Vocabulary Knowledge and III. Comprehension

Directions: Read the section in your text entitled "Building Our Capital City" (pages 60–63). Using the information from your reading, answer the questions below on a separate sheet of paper.

II. Vocabulary Knowledge
   8. Define the term *district* as used in this text (page 62).
   9. What do the letters *DC* stand for in Washington, DC?
   10. Define the term *capital city*. Provide two examples of capital cities.
   11. In the following sentence, what does the word *founded* mean? "The United States was *founded* more than 200 years ago."

III. Comprehension
   12. In how many cities was our capital located? Name them.
   13. Why did the leaders choose the area they did to put the capital?
   14. Why did the people need a city specially built to be the nation's capital?
   15. Look at the time chart on page 63. Was the White House built before or after the Washington Monument?
   16. On the map on page 61, use the key to locate the Lincoln Memorial. On what street is it located? What building is directly east of the Lincoln Memorial?

ACTIVITY

DEVELOPING A CONTENT READING INVENTORY

The purpose of this exercise is to provide practice in developing a content reading inventory.

Directions: Locate a textbook used in intermediate elementary grades or middle school, and create a content reading inventory following the guidelines given on previous pages. If possible, administer the inventory and report the results using the criteria on page 140.

THE GROUP READING INVENTORY

The *group reading inventory (GRI)* is a useful procedure for identifying students who may have difficulty comprehending the content of a textbook. In addition, it can be used to approximate a student's instructional reading level. The GRI is appropriate for students in grade 3 or higher and can be administered orally with readers in grades 2 and 3.

The teacher uses the **directed reading activity (DRA)** format for instruction in administering the GRI. There are three phases to the DRA: introduction (background development), silent reading, and comprehension check. In the background development phase, the teacher questions students to assess their background knowledge on the topic. The teacher introduces vocabulary from the text and also develops a purpose for reading. In the second phase, the students read silently. The teacher should observe students' silent reading behaviors; many teachers use a structured observation form (see Chapter 3) on selected students. Finally, students respond to the comprehension questions. The teacher then collects the written work and leads an oral discussion on the passage.

From this procedure, the teacher can make estimations on students' abilities to read the text. Specific questions can provide hints about students' comprehension strategies, such as predicting and using context to gain meaning.

To score the GRI, use the following criteria (Rakes & Smith, 1986):

Percent Correct Responses to GRI Questions

80–100% = student will find the textbook easy to read

65–79%   = student will need some assistance to read and understand the text

below 65% = student will find the text too difficult and will need considerable assistance and supplemental help to use the text

Example of a Group Reading Inventory (Grade 4)

I. Introduction (background development)

Ask students to look at a picture depicting South America. Discuss the following questions with the students:

What do you think you might see in South America?
What plants grow in South America?

II. Silent Reading

Give the passage on South America (p. 143) to students, and say:

"This passage is part of a chapter from your book on South America. Let's read to get introduced to South America and find some interesting facts. If you come to a word you do not know, raise your hand, and I will help you. Now read silently so that you can answer questions when you are done. When you have completed the reading, turn the paper over."

III. Comprehension Check

Give the comprehension questions (see below) to the students, and say:

> "Now you will write the answers to the questions dealing with the passage on South America. Answer completely. Try to write something for all the questions. You may look back at the passage. When you are finished, turn your paper over."

IV. Follow-up Discussion

Collect the students' papers and discuss the questions orally. This discussion will provide an opportunity to evaluate the students' oral language and also to give the students feedback on the correct answers to the questions.

Reading Passage

South America

The continent of South America has twelve nations. Brazil is the largest country. It takes up almost half of the continent. The continent is bordered by both the Atlantic and the Pacific oceans.

Much of the center of South America is wilderness. About half of the people live in cities. But the big cities are near the oceans. Outside the cities, most of the people are farmers. They grow coffee, cacao (which makes chocolate), sugar cane, and bananas.

South America has some interesting places. The driest place in the world is the Atacama Desert in Chile. It's so dry, no one has ever seen rain fall in the desert. The largest rain forest is also found in South America. In the rain forest, trees grow so close together that sunlight never reaches the ground. And the longest mountain range in the world, the Andes, is in South America.

Comprehension Questions

1. How many countries are in South America?

2. Where do most of the people live?

3. What is a desert?

4. How are the Atacama Desert and the rain forest different? How are they alike?

5.   What do you want to learn about South America?

6.   Summarize the reading.

7.   We have studied several continents and countries located in them. Predict some words that might be found in the chapter on South America.

A C T I V I T Y

GROUP READING INVENTORY

The purpose of this activity is for you to interpret the results of a group reading inventory and recommend some instructional strategies for the teaching of the unit.

Directions: A fifth grade class completed the group reading inventory shown on page 145. The teacher, Mrs. Bullard, scored the children's answers to the comprehension questions and summarized the results, which are given below.

Examine the results and answer the following questions:

1.   What comprehension problems might Mrs. Bullard encounter in teaching the unit?

2.   What hypotheses about the students are likely?

3.   How could Mrs. Bullard introduce the unit and enhance comprehension?

4.   What reading strategies appear to need strengthening by a number of the students?

Results of Group Reading Inventory
Comprehension Questions

1. How many countries are in South America?
   15 - correct
   10 - incorrect

2. Where do most of the people in South America live?
   12 - correct
   13 - incorrect

3. What is a desert?
   20 - correct
   5 - incorrect

4. How are the Atacama Desert and the rain forest different? How are they alike?
   5 - correct
   15 - incorrect
   5 - no response

5. What do you want to learn about South America?
   17 - no response
   8 - responded with different answers: Do the children go to school? What games do they play? Do they have Thanksgiving? Is it hot there? Do people live in the desert? What do they eat? Can we have pen pals? What kind of animals do they have?

6. Summarize the reading.
   8 - gave adequate summary
   10 - gave incomplete summaries
   7 - no response

7. We have studied several continents and countries. Predict some words that might be found in the chapter on South America and write them below.
   23 - no response
   2 - gave different responses: Spanish, cowboys, tacos, llama

STRATEGIES FOR EVALUATING METACOGNITIVE COMPREHENSION SKILLS

Metacognition is the learner's ability to know how to learn and how to evaluate his or her learning. Metacognitive strategies can be divided into four phases of approaching a task: *planning, strategy execution, monitoring,* and *evaluating.*

In the planning phase, the reader analyzes the task required of him or her. Questions that guide this phase may be the following:

What kind of reading material is it?

What do I already know about the subject?

What do I expect to learn?

What is the task, or my goal?

What do I think is going to happen in the story?

In the strategy-execution phase, the reader selects a suitable strategy that will allow him or her to realize a learning goal. The reader may elect to skim the passage and develop a set of guiding questions, as in survey, question, read, recite, review (**SQ3R**). Or the reader may use a strategy appropriate for a text structure, such as story grammar or a pattern guide. **Imaging** or notetaking are other strategies the reader may select. In other words, the reader initiates the reading task with the most appropriate strategy to facilitate the meaning-making process.

In the third phase, students who use metacognitive strategies monitor the reading/learning process by consciously summarizing and clarifying what they read. They have strategies available to determine unknown words, and they may employ text reinspection, or *look backs*, in an effort to monitor comprehension. In this phase, the reader is actively engaged in checking his or her level of understanding and using repair strategies when comprehension fails.

When the reading/learning task is complete, the student enters the fourth phase, evaluation. In this phase, questions that guide the learner may be the following:

What did I learn?

Did I complete the task?

Am I satisfied with my level of learning?

What do I still need to know?

Thus, metacognitive strategies help readers gain conscious control of their reading and learning behaviors. These are important skills to the development of independent learners and good comprehenders.

Reciprocal Teaching

Reciprocal teaching (Palincsar & Brown, 1985) is a technique designed to develop the student's comprehension and metacomprehension skills. As a diagnostic technique, reciprocal teaching examines the student's ability to predict, question, and summarize, which are metacognitive skills.

Reciprocal teaching is conducted with a small group using content material. The teacher first explains the steps in the process. Used in instruction, the teacher models the procedure several times and takes the lead in directing the discussion. When the students are comfortable with the procedure, they take turns serving as the group leader, or "teacher." Thus, the term *reciprocal teaching.*

The procedure consists of four reading-thinking processes:

1. Prediction: The reader predicts from the title, headings, and illustrations what the reading is about or what will happen next.
2. Question: The reader constructs good questions to guide the reading.
3. Clarification: The reader looks for difficult vocabulary, unclear and/or incomplete information, and unusual language.
4. Summarization: The reader identifies the topic, develops a main idea sentence with one or two details, and derives a conclusion sentence.

When used in assessment, a written guide, rather than the oral exercise, may be employed. The written guide on pages 149-150 is used for such a purpose.

In evaluating a student's performance on a reciprocal teaching exercise, the teacher uses the following questions to identify behaviors:

1. Can the student use cues to determine the topic or subject matter?
2. Is the student able to formulate questions to guide the reading?
3. Are the students' questions low or high level?
4. Does the student make an effort to clarify unknown words? In his or her attempt to clarify, does the student use context?
5. Does the student summarize the passage by including a main idea statement?

RECIPROCAL TEACHING GUIDE

Directions: Follow the steps below in order. **R** before the direction means you will read. **W** means you will write the answer to a question. To complete this assignment, you will read pages _____ in your text.

R   Read the title of the section and subtitles. Then skim the first paragraph.

W   What is this going to be about?

_____

_____

_____

W   What are two questions you have on this topic that can guide your reading?

_____

_____

R   Now read the first section.

W   What words were unfamiliar to you?

_____

_____

W   What do you think those words mean?

_____

_____

W What was unclear to you as you read this passage?

_____

_____

W Write a summary of this section.

_____

_____

_____

_____

Prediction Guide

A **prediction guide** is a written informal assessment that determines whether a student uses schemata, or background knowledge, in making predictions and whether a student can make inferences.

The teacher selects a chapter from a content textbook and uses the chapter title, subtitles, and key terms to develop the guide, such as that presented below.

Additional questions to be used with such a guide may include, but not be limited to, the following:

1. What do you think this chapter will be about?
2. What makes you think so?
3. What do you already know about this subject?
4. What words do you think will be used in this chapter?
5. What question(s) could guide your reading of this chapter?

In evaluating a student's performance, the teacher uses the following questions to identify behaviors:

1. Can the student make valid predictions about the topic or subject matter?
2. Is the student able to formulate questions to guide the reading?
3. Are the student's questions low or high level?
4. What is the student's level of background knowledge?
5. Does the student use background knowledge to make valid predictions?

Example of a Prediction Guide

Directions: Read the title and subtitle below.

The People of a Metropolitan Community
People, People Everywhere!

What do you think a chapter with this title will be about?

_____

Now read the remaining subtitles listed below:

    What Kinds of People?
    The Basic Group: The Family
    Education and Religion
    Recreation

What are three major ideas that might be presented in this chapter?

1. _____

2. _____

3. _____

Which of the following words might appear in this chapter? Check (✓) the ones you think you will meet.

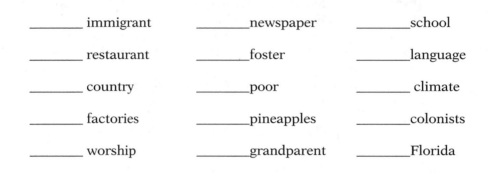

_____ immigrant	_____ newspaper	_____ school
_____ restaurant	_____ foster	_____ language
_____ country	_____ poor	_____ climate
_____ factories	_____ pineapples	_____ colonists
_____ worship	_____ grandparent	_____ Florida

ReQuest Procedure

The **ReQuest Procedure** (Manzo, 1970) is appropriate for all levels of students, kindergarten through college, and can be used in a group setting as well as with individual students. It is a teaching technique designed to promote active comprehension through self-questioning, developing purposes for reading, and making predictions. The teacher can assess the student's ability to perform the following tasks:

1. formulate questions about material being read
2. answer questions
3. adopt an active inquiring attitude toward reading
4. follow the question-answering behavior pattern

The following outline describes the method for constructing and administering a ReQuest procedure.

1. The teacher selects a text that is at the student's instructional reading level and that is predictive in nature. Narrative text is particularly suited for this procedure.
2. Before the lesson, the teacher identifies appropriate stopping points in the text for asking questions.
3. To prepare students for the reading, the teacher should
   a. build interest in the reading material
   b. introduce vocabulary
   c. develop background or concepts
4. The teacher provides the following guidelines at the start of ReQuest:

   "The purpose of this lesson is to improve your understanding of what you read. We will each read a section (paragraph) silently. Then we will take turns asking questions. You will ask questions first, then I will ask questions. Try to ask the kinds of questions a teacher might ask.

   "You may ask me as many questions as you wish on the material. While you are asking me questions, I will close my book. When I ask you questions, you will close your book.

I don't know is not an acceptable answer. If a question is unclear, we can ask for clarity, and the questioner must rephrase the question. If we need to, we can open the text and look back for the answer."

5. The teacher and students read silently the assigned section.

6. The teacher closes the book, and the students ask questions. The teacher answers the questions and models look backs and mental reasoning.

7. The teacher and students read silently the next section, and then the teacher asks the questions. The teacher should, when appropriate, attempt to elicit predictions and validations from the students by prompting "What do you think will happen? Why do you think so? Read the line that proves it."

8. The procedure may be repeated again. Then the students read the rest of the story silently. The teacher can use a follow-up discussion and extension activities.

In evaluating students' responses, the teacher uses the following questions to identify behaviors:

1. Did some students have difficulty forming questions?

2. Did the students ask questions on different levels of comprehension?

3. Were students' predictions valid?

4. Did students answer the teacher's questions appropriately?

ACTIVITY

EVALUATING METACOGNITIVE COMPREHENSION STRATEGIES

Directions: Select either reciprocal teaching, prediction guide, or ReQuest procedure, and conduct an evaluation of one student's comprehension strategies. Use the Observation Checklist: Metacognitive Strategies (p. 155) to record the student's responses. Write a summary of your findings and at least two suggestions for future reading instruction.

OBSERVATION CHECKLIST
METACOGNITIVE STRATEGIES

Student _____ Grade _____

Examiner _____

	Obs. I Date _____		Obs. II Date _____	
	DA*	NI*	DA*	NI*
1. Links prior knowledge before reading.	_____	_____	_____	_____
2. Develops purpose for reading.	_____	_____	_____	_____
3. Uses titles and/or illustrations to predict content/events.	_____	_____	_____	_____
4. Verifies predictions.	_____	_____	_____	_____
5. Develops questions to guide reading.	_____	_____	_____	_____
6. Creates visual representations of key concepts (web, outline, etc.).	_____	_____	_____	_____
7. Summarizes.	_____	_____	_____	_____

Summary

_____

_____

_____

_____

Recommendations

_____

_____

_____

_____

*DA = Developing Adequately.

 NI = Needs Improvement.

STRATEGIES FOR EVALUATING COMPREHENSION OF STORY STRUCTURE

Story Maps

A **story map** is a visual representation of the key elements in a narrative text. These elements are setting, the main character(s), the problem, the main character's goal, the plot or events, and the resolution.

The teacher selects a narrative passage and discusses the organization of a story. Using the story map (see page 159), the teacher explains each element of the story.

Then the students read the story and complete the map, writing the appropriate answer in each box. When used for diagnostic purposes, the maps are collected and a group discussion takes place. During instruction, teacher and students complete the maps together. Rather than working with the entire map, the teacher may concentrate on one aspect, such as the plot or problem. In assessment, the teacher can evaluate entire maps completed by individual students to assess the student's knowledge of story structure.

In evaluating a student's performance, the teacher uses the following questions to identify behaviors:

1. Can the student determine the setting?
2. Can the student state the problem?
3. Can the student recognize the main characters?
4. Does the student provide the events in sequential order? Are the events given critical to the story?
5. Can the student identify the resolution?

STORY MAP FORM

The Setting

Where and when does the story take place?

Main Characters

Who are the people in the story?

The Problem

The Main Character's Goal

What does the Main Character want to do?

The Plot - What happened?

Event 1

Event 2

Event 3

Event 4

The Resolution

How did it end?

Story Frames

Another way to assess story grammar is to provide a story frame. A story frame consists of a series of incomplete sentences that deal with the elements of a story. After students read a story, they fill in the blank spaces in the "frames." Oral discussion can either precede or follow the story frame activity. Evaluation of students' responses on the story frame should include an examination of the students' knowledge of story structure and comprehension of the story.

The story frame provided on page 163 is generic and can be utilized with any story. Story frames can be constructed for specific selections, focus on a particular character, or strengthen a comprehension strategy (comparison, sequence, cause-effect).

STORY FRAME* FORM

Student _____ Date _____

Title _____

Author _____ Genre _____

The main character in this story is _____

_____

The supporting characters are _____

_____

The story takes place _____

_____

The problem in the story is _____

_____

_____

_____

Some of the major events are _____

_____

_____

_____

_____

_____

_____

_____

*Developed by R. Howard Blount (personal communication, January 1991). Reprinted with permission.

(major events cont.) _____

_____

_____

The problem is solved when _____

_____

_____

_____

The author's message is _____

_____

_____

_____

The message makes me think _____

_____

_____

_____

I (liked / did not like) this story because _____

_____

_____

_____

_____

Forms for Assessing Progress Using Story Maps and Story Frames

Students' knowledge of story structure can be recorded onto record sheets, which can assist the teacher in determining needed instructional areas as well as monitoring students' progress. Two such forms are provided on pages 167 and 169.

The *Literary Elements Individual Record* is completed on an individual child, is maintained over time, and should be included in a child's portfolio or reading file. The *Literary Elements Class Record* maps the needs of the entire class or of a small group of children. After reviewing a child's responses to the story map or story frame, the teacher judges if the child has developed the concept by marking DA (Developing Adequately), NI (Needs Improvement), or NO (Concept Not Observed) in the appropriate spaces on the record.

These forms are only samples; you may want to develop your own record keeping system as well as evaluation codes.

LITERARY ELEMENTS
INDIVIDUAL RECORD*

Student _____ Date _____

Date	Title	Charac-ter	Setting	Problem	Event	Solution	Theme	Applica-tion	Re-sponse

Key:
DA = Developing Adequately
NI = Needs Improvement
NO = Not Observed

*Developed by R. Howard Blount (personal communication, January 1991). Reprinted with permission.

LITERARY ELEMENTS
CLASS RECORD*

Title _____ Date _____

Student	Charac-ter	Setting	Problem	Event	Solution	Theme	Applica-tion	Re-sponse

Key:
DA = Developing Adequately
NI = Needs Improvement
NO = Not Observed

*Developed by R. Howard Blount (personal communication, January 1991). Reprinted with permission.

Story Retelling

Story retellings can also be used to evaluate a student's awareness of story structure and sequence.

In **story retelling,** the student reads or listens to a story and then orally recalls what he or she remembers. Retelling should be assessed several times during the year. With the use of this evaluation tool, growth in the child's knowledge of story structure, sequence, and details can be documented.

Before conducting a retelling, the teacher describes to the student the purpose and procedure of the task. During the retelling, the teacher should not prompt the child other than to say, "Can you think of anything else?"

A quantitative analysis sheet for the retelling* provides for examination of the student's knowledge of the structural elements in a story: setting, theme, plot, and resolution. The teacher notes the different story elements regardless of the order in which the child recounted them (Morrow, 1988).

Retelling should be taught, and children should be provided practice. As a teaching technique, it can help develop a child's comprehension, sense of story structure, and oral language skills. As an assessment technique, retelling provides insight into the child's ability to recall details and make inferences.

SAMPLE
Story Retelling: A Quantitative Analysis

The following is a sample retelling of "The Three Bears" by a first-grade child along with a completed quantitative scoring sheet.

> Goldilocks went to the three bears' house and ate the porridge. Then she broke the baby bear's chair. Then she went to the beds. "Too hard," she said. "Too soft," she said. "Just right." And she went to sleep and the bears came home and she ran away.

I. Sense of Story Structure
- a. Begins story with an introduction   _0_
- b. Names main character   _1_
- c. Number of other characters named   _3_
- d. Actual number of other characters   _3_
- e. Score for other characters (c/d)   _1_
- f. Includes statement about time or place   _0_

II. Theme

Refers to main character's primary goal or

problem to be solved   _0_

III. Plot Episodes
- a. Number of episodes recalled   _7_
- b. Number of episodes in story   _9_
- c. Score for plot episodes (a/b)   _.8_

*Appendix B and C, "Retelling Stories as a Diagnostic Tool," Lesley M. Morrow, *Reexamining Reading Diagnosis*, Susan Mandel Glazer, Lyndon W. Searfoss, and Lance M. Gentile (Eds.), 1988, pp. 142–145. Reprinted with permission of Lesley M. Morrow and the International Reading Association.

IV. Resolution
   a. Names problem solution/goal attainment   _0_
   b. Ends story   _1_

V. Sequence
   Retells story in structural order: setting,
   theme, plot episodes, resolution. (Score 2
   for proper, 1 for partial, 0 for no sequence
   evident.)   _2_

Highest score possible: _10_   Student's score _5.8_

Interpretation
The child did not begin with an introduction, did not mention the setting
(forest), and omitted the reason Goldilocks went to the house (she was tired
and wanted to rest). The child did name all the characters and recalled seven of
the nine events in proper sequence. Instruction for this child should focus on
the identification of the setting, problem, and resolution. The child does have a
good sense of story sequence, even though some details were left out.

```
A C T I V I T Y
```

EVALUATING COMPREHENSION OF
STORY STRUCTURE

Directions: Evaluate a student's or small group of students' knowledge of
story structure using either story maps, story frames, or story retelling. Use the
following Quantitative Analysis Sheet and write a summary of your findings,
along with two suggestions for further reading instruction.

QUANTITATIVE ANALYSIS SHEET
Story Retelling

I. Sense of Story Structure
    a. Begins story with an introduction   _____
    b. Names main character   _____
    c. Number of other characters named   _____
    d. Actual number of other characters   _____
    e. Score for other characters (c/d)   _____
    f. Includes statement about time or place   _____

II. Theme
Refers to main character's primary goal or
problem to be solved   _____

III. Plot Episodes
    a. Number of episodes recalled   _____
    b. Number of episodes in story   _____
    c. Score for plot episodes (a/b)   _____

IV. Resolution
    a. Names problem solution/goal attainment   _____
    b. Ends story   _____

V. Sequence
Retells story in structural order: setting,
theme, plot episodes, resolution. (Score 2
for proper, 1 for partial, 0 for no sequence
evident.)   _____

Highest score possible: _____   Student's score _____

SUMMARY

The evaluation of comprehension strategies and skills can be conducted through informal measures such as the cloze test and a content reading inventory. This chapter offered practice in interpreting data from these informal measures as well as instructional practices combined with observation. These methods may be the most useful in the classroom assessment process.

SUGGESTED READINGS

Glazer, S., & Searfoss, L. (1988). *Reading diagnosis and instruction: A C-A-L-M approach.* Englewood Cliffs, NJ: Prentice Hall.

Marzano, R. J., Hagerty, P. J., Valencia, S. W., & DiStefano, P. P. (1987). *Reading diagnosis and instruction: Theory into practice.* Englewood Cliffs, NJ: Prentice Hall.

Muth, K. D. (Ed.). (1989). *Children's comprehension of text: Research and practice.* Newark, NJ: International Reading Association.

Richek, M. A., List, Lynne K., & Lerner, J. W. (1989). *Reading problems: Assessment and teaching strategies* (2nd ed.). Englewood Cliffs, NJ: Prentice Hall.

Tierney, R. J., Readence, J. E., & Dishner, E. K. (1985). *Reading strategies and practices: A compendium* (2nd ed.). Boston: Allyn & Bacon.

Walker, B. J. (1988). *Diagnostic teaching of reading: Techniques for instruction and assessment.* Columbus, OH: Merrill Publishing Company.

CHAPTER 8

ASSESSMENT OF WORD-RECOGNITION KNOWLEDGE AND SPELLING STAGES

It may be necessary to gain more insight and information about a child's word-recognition strategies and knowledge of **phonemic awareness**. This is often the case when a child is unable to read connected text or reads more than one year below current grade placement. Determining how a student deals with individual words and sounds in words will provide useful information to facilitate reading instruction.

This chapter presents a variety of tests for word recognition that can be individually administered in a short time period. Additionally, a method of analyzing spelling stages is given. These stages have been linked to reading development and can provide additional insight into a child's instructional strengths and needs. As with the other assessment techniques presented in this text, these measures should be administered several times during the year to measure growth and assess needs.

ASSESSING WORD-ANALYSIS SKILLS

One method of assessing word-analysis ability is an *informal word-analysis test*. The test is given individually, and the teacher should observe for strategies as well as strengths and weaknesses. An informal word-analysis test can include any of the following:

1. phonic principles
2. **structural-analysis** knowledge
3. alphabet knowledge
4. blending skills

Some tests use real words, while others use only nonsense words. The test discussed in this chapter uses both nonsense and real words.

There are several published tests designed for measuring word-analysis skills. However, *a word-analysis test is easy to construct and can be designed to correlate with the reading curriculum.* The teacher is encouraged to examine commercially made tests and informal-type tests to see which is best suited to the curriculum used in the classroom.

The Klesius-Homan Phonic Word-analysis Test*

The *Klesius-Homan Phonic Word-analysis Test* is an example of an informal word-analysis test. The following is a breakdown of the abilities measured in each section:

Section I	Initial consonant sounds
	Final consonant sounds
	Consonant vowel consonant (CVC) short vowel sounds in isolation and in context
Section II	Initial consonant digraphs and blends
	Final consonant digraphs and blends
Section III	Final *e*
	Initial consonant blends
Section IV	Vowel diphthongs
	Vowels modified by *R*
	Vowels digraphs *A*
Section V	Syllabication
	Blending

Instructions for Administering the Test

1. The examiner reads to the student the directions in each section.
2. To begin, the examiner asks the student to read the three words in Section IA. If the student is unable to read the words, the examiner should pronounce the words for the student. The student then reads the words in Section IB.
3. The examiner records what the child says for each word.
4. If the student is unable to read any word in Section IB, the examiner proceeds to Section IC.
5. Continue administering Sections II through V. Administration of the test is stopped if the student misses one-half or more of the items in two successive sections of the test.
6. In some sections, real and nonsense words are given. The real words are to be used first. If the student does not successfully read one-half or more of the real words, do not proceed to the nonsense words.
7. The group of words in each section should be placed on separate 5-by-7 cards so that only one group is presented to the child at a time.

*Klesius and Homan (1980). Reprinted with permission.

THE KLESIUS-HOMAN PHONIC WORD-ANALYSIS TEST

Section I

A. Read these words.

an   it   am

B. Read the following words.

bit	can	fit	jam
Dan	Kit	lit	gam
hit	wit	van	man
Nan	quit	tan	sit
ran	pan		

cham	chin	wham	slam
sham	shin	whip	scram
flat	cram	Stan	
blip	trip	strip	

C. Give a sound for the beginning letter in each word.

Section II

A. Read these words.

lad	lip	bog	hum	pep
lack	disk	shop	chug	rest

dag	lig	wot	hup	ped
shap	dilp	chad	stug	leck

B. Read these sentences.

1. Her red hat had a rip in the top.

2. The hen ran from the big fat hog.

3. Greg hit his chin when he fell from the crib.

4. The duck went to rest in his nest by the pond.

5. Chip had a wish to catch a big fish.

Section III

Read these words.

gate	time	bone	mule
plate	shine	globe	cute

sate	dibe	rone	cupe
slace	flime	plote	spute

Section IV

Read these words.

seen	soak	leaf	paid
queen	cloak	dream	chain

howl	toil	coy	couch
towp	foin	loy	lound
laud	part	berth	lurk
juat	barm	sert	nurk
thirst	drawn	shirp	tawp

Section V

Read these words.

candy	dishes	excitement
tumble	happen	transportable
shipmate	basket	undefeated
locate	reload	reconstruction
table	label	

lanry	loshes	mealment
dunble	dippen	translotable
hipsat	tisket	readventing
topate	retoad	discabination
rable	nodel	

SAMPLE
Klesius-Homan Phonic
Word-analysis Test

Student _Becky_ Grade _1_

Section I

A. Read these words.

an   it   am

B. Read the following words.

✓ * bit	✓ can	✓ fit	✓ jam
✓ Dan	✓ Kit	✓ lit	_grāme_ gam
✓ hit	✓ wit	✓ van	✓ man
✓ Nan	_cute_ quit	✓ tan	✓ sit
✓ ran	_pin_ pan		

kam cham	_can_ chin	_NR_ † wham	_sam_ slam
jam sham	_sin_ shin	_NR_ whip	_NR_ scram
✓ flat	_crāne_ cram	_stand_ Stan	
✓ blip	_tip_ trip	_NR_ strip	

C. Give a sound for the beginning letter in each word.

Section II

A. Read these words.

✓ lad	✓ lip	_dog_ bog	✓ hum	_pip_ pep
luck lack	_dis_ disk	_stop_ shop	_NR_ chug	_NR_ rest

dig dag	✓ lig	_wōte_ wot	✓ hup	_pid_ ped
sap shap	_bilp_ dilp	_sāde_ chad	✓ stug	_lig_ leck

*Word read correctly.

†No Response.

B. Read these sentences.

1. *Here* ✓ ✓ ✓ ✓ ✓ ✓ *NR*
    Her red hat had a rip in the top.

2. ✓ ✓ ✓ ✓ ✓ ✓ ✓ *NR*
    The hen ran from the big fat hog.

3. *NR* ✓ ✓ *NR* ✓ ✓ ✓ ✓ ✓ *sib.*
    Greg hit his chin when he fell from the crib.

4. ✓ ✓ ✓ ✓ ✓ ✓ ✓ *needs* ✓ ✓ *pan.*
    The duck went to rest in his nest by the pond.

5. *NR* ✓ ✓ *NR* ✓ *NR* ✓ ✓ *NR*
    Chip had a wish to catch a big fish.

Section III

Read these words.

got	✓	✓	✓
gate	time	bone	mule
pilt	*NR*	*NR*	*cut*
plate	shine	globe	cute

sat	*bid*	*NR*	*cud*
sate	dibe	rone	cupe
NR	*film*	*polt*	*sōte*
slace	flime	plote	spute

Section IV

Read these words.   *Not administered*

seen	soak	leaf	paid
queen	cloak	dream	chain

howl	toil	coy	couch
towp	foin	loy	lound
laud	part	berth	lurk
juat	barm	sert	nurk
thirst	drawn	shirp	tawp

Section V

Read these words.   *Not administered*

candy	dishes	excitement
tumble	happen	transportable
shipmate	basket	undefeated
locate	reload	reconstruction
table	label	

lanry	loshes	mealment
dunble	dippen	translotable
hipsat	tisket	readventing
topate	retoad	discabination
rable	nodel	

Interpretation

Becky has had difficulty completing her assignments this year. When asked to read orally, she would often show confusion as to where to begin and would lose her place. The *Klesius-Homan Phonic Word-analysis Test* indicated Becky knew beginning and ending sounds but had considerable difficulty with consonant blends, digraphs, and vowels. She showed more difficulty with the nonsense words, which may indicate she relies on sight vocabulary.

A C T I V I T Y

USING THE KLESIUS-HOMAN PHONIC
WORD-ANALYSIS TEST

Directions: Using the marked test below, analyze the child's reading strengths and weaknesses.

Student ___*Antonio*___ Grade ___*2*___

Section I

A. Read these words.

an   it   am

B. Read the following words.

dit bit	✓* can	✓ fit	*jan* jam
✓ Dan	*cat* Kit	✓ lit	*game* gam
it hit	*with* wit	✓ van	✓ man
✓ Nan	*cit* quit	✓ tan	✓ sit
✓ ran	✓ pan		

sam cham	*sin* chin	*ham* wham	*slam* slam
san sham	*him* shin	*hip* whip	*kam* scram
flat flat	*kam* cram	*san* Stan	
bip blip	*tip* trip	*sip* strip	

C. Give a sound for the beginning letter in each word.

Section II

A. Read these words.

✓ lad	✓ lip	*bag* bog	*him* hum	✓ pep
lat lack	*dis* disk	*NR* [†] shop	*NR* chug	✓ rest

*Word read correctly.

[†]No Response.

✓	*lip*	*wol*	*hip*	✓
dag	lig	wot	hup	ped
sap	*dil*	✓	*stung*	✓
shap	dilp	chad	stug	leck

B. Read these sentences.

1. Her red hat had a rip in the top.   [✓ ✓ ✓ ✓ ✓ ✓ ✓ ✓]

2. The hen ran from the big fat hog.   [✓ ✓ ✓ ✓ ✓ ✓ ✓ ✓]

3. Greg hit his chin when he fell from the crib.   [*NR* ✓ ✓ *cap* ✓ ✓ ✓ ✓ ✓ *sib.*]

4. The duck went to rest in his nest by the pond.   [✓ ✓ ✓ ✓ ✓ ✓ ✓ *net* ✓ ✓ *pod*]

5. Chip had a wish to catch a big fish.   [✓ ✓ ✓ ✓ ✓ ✓✓ ✓]

Section III

Read these words.   *Not administered*

gate	time	bone	mule
plate	shine	globe	cute

sate	dibe	rone	cupe
slace	flime	plote	spute

Section IV

Read these words.   *Not administered*

seen	soak	leaf	paid
queen	cloak	dream	chain

howl	toil	coy	couch
towp	foin	loy	lound
laud	part	berth	lurk
juat	barm	sert	nurk
thirst	drawn	shirp	tawp

Section V

Read these words.   *Not administered*

candy	dishes	excitement
tumble	happen	transportable
shipmate	basket	undefeated
locate	reload	reconstruction
table	lable	

lanry	loshes	mealment
dunble	dippen	translotable
hipsat	tisket	readventing
topate	retoad	discabination
rable	nodel	

Analysis of Strengths and Weaknesses

_____

_____

_____

_____

_____

_____

_____

_____

_____

_____

Assessing Sight Word Knowledge: The Fry Instant Word Lists

The use of **sight words** is a key strategy for word recognition. Sight words are those words the reader can rapidly identify without using word-analysis strategies, such as phonics, context clues, or structural analysis. Together, word-analysis and -recognition strategies allow the reader to concentrate on the comprehension of text. Word recognition is a basic strategy: if a child is unable to read connected text at a grade one level, the teacher should investigate the level of word-recognition and word-analysis skills the child has acquired.

The *Fry Instant Word Lists* (Fry, 1980) are composed of high-frequency sight words. Fry states that the first 100 Instant Words make up 65 percent of all written text. Obviously, instant recognition of these words assists the reader in both comprehension and enjoyment. The Fry Lists have been adapted here as an informal assessment for sight word knowledge with children who are having difficulty reading connected text at the grade one level.

```
A C T I V I T Y
```

USING THE FRY INSTANT WORD LISTS*

This assessment is administered individually.

Directions: Provide the child with the student copy of the Fry Instant Word Lists. Say: "You will read aloud from these lists. I want you to read down each column, starting with list #1. Some of the words you may not know. If that happens, just say 'pass.' " We recommend that you reveal only one column of words at a time by covering the other columns with a 5 by 8 card.

Place a "+" sign in the first column of your evaluation form if the child reads the word correctly or a "–" if the child reads it incorrectly. Write the child's response in the space provided next to the word if it is read incorrectly. If the child passes or does not respond, mark NR (no response) in this space. Administer consecutive lists until the child reads less than 75 percent correct, or less than 18 words on the list.

Students who score less than 75 percent correct on any of the four Instant Lists should be provided instruction with sight words; shared reading experiences with big books; guided writing activities, such as LEA; and multiple experiences with print.

---

*"The new instant word lists" Edward B. Fry, *The Reading Teacher*, December 1980. Reprinted with permission of the International Reading Association.

FRY'S INSTANT WORD LISTS
Student Copy

I	II	III	IV
the	or	will	number
of	one	up	no
and	had	other	way
a	by	about	could
to	word	out	people
in	but	many	my
is	not	then	than
you	what	them	first
that	all	these	water
it	were	so	been
he	we	some	call
was	when	her	who
for	your	would	oil
on	can	make	now
are	said	like	find
as	there	him	long
with	use	into	down
his	an	time	day
they	each	has	did
I	which	look	get
at	she	two	come
be	do	more	made
this	how	write	may
have	their	go	part
from	if	see	over

FRY'S INSTANT WORD LIST I
Evaluation Form

Child's Name _____ Grade _____

Date _____ Examiner _____

Correct? + −	Word	Child's Response	Correct? + −	Word	Child's Response
_____	the	_____	_____	at	_____
_____	of	_____	_____	be	_____
_____	and	_____	_____	this	_____
_____	a	_____	_____	have	_____
_____	to	_____	_____	from	_____
_____	in	_____			
_____	is	_____			
_____	you	_____			
_____	that	_____			
_____	it	_____			
_____	he	_____			
_____	was	_____			
_____	for	_____			
_____	on	_____			
_____	are	_____			
_____	as	_____			
_____	with	_____			
_____	his	_____			
_____	they	_____			
_____	I	_____		Correct = _____ / 25 = _____ %	

FRY'S INSTANT WORD LIST II
Evaluation Form

Child's Name _____ Grade _____

Date _____ Examiner _____

Correct? + −	Word	Child's Response	Correct? + −	Word	Child's Response
———	or	———————	———	she	———————
———	one	———————	———	do	———————
———	had	———————	———	how	———————
———	by	———————	———	their	———————
———	word	———————	———	if	———————
———	but	———————			
———	not	———————			
———	what	———————			
———	all	———————			
———	were	———————			
———	we	———————			
———	when	———————			
———	your	———————			
———	can	———————			
———	said	———————			
———	there	———————			
———	use	———————			
———	an	———————			
———	each	———————			
———	which	———————			

Correct = _____ / 25 = _____ %

FRY'S INSTANT WORD LIST III
Evaluation Form

Child's Name _____ Grade _____

Date _____ Examiner _____

Correct? + −	Word	Child's Response	Correct? + −	Word	Child's Response
_____	will	_____	_____	two	_____
_____	up	_____	_____	more	_____
_____	other	_____	_____	write	_____
_____	about	_____	_____	go	_____
_____	out	_____	_____	see	_____
_____	many	_____			
_____	then	_____			
_____	them	_____			
_____	these	_____			
_____	so	_____			
_____	some	_____			
_____	her	_____			
_____	would	_____			
_____	make	_____			
_____	like	_____			
_____	him	_____			
_____	into	_____			
_____	time	_____			
_____	has	_____			
_____	look	_____	Correct = _____ / 25 = _____ %

FRY'S INSTANT WORD LIST IV
Evaluation Form

Child's Name _____ Grade _____

Date _____ Examiner _____

Correct? + –	Word	Child's Response	Correct? + –	Word	Child's Response
_____	number	_____	_____	come	_____
_____	no	_____	_____	made	_____
_____	way	_____	_____	may	_____
_____	could	_____	_____	part	_____
_____	people	_____	_____	over	_____
_____	my	_____			
_____	than	_____			
_____	first	_____			
_____	water	_____			
_____	been	_____			
_____	call	_____			
_____	who	_____			
_____	oil	_____			
_____	now	_____			
_____	find	_____			
_____	long	_____			
_____	down	_____			
_____	day	_____			
_____	did	_____			
_____	get	_____	Correct = _____ / 25 = _____ %

Assessing Phonemic Awareness

In order to match sounds in a spoken word to letters in a printed word, a reader must be able to hear and separate each phoneme (speech sound) in the word. This process is called *phonemic segmentation.*

Gillet and Temple (1990) report that phonemic segmentation is difficult at the emergent reading level for many children. However, the ability to segment words into phonemes has been recognized as an important skill for both reading and writing.

Stahl and Murray (1993) found a relationship between the phoneme isolation task and reading preprimer words in isolation. There was also a strong correlation between phonological awareness and spelling ability. They concluded that "knowledge of letter names might enable children to separate onsets from rimes,[1] which, in turn, would enable basic word recognition. Basic word recognition might enable more complex forms of phonological awareness..." (p. 20).

The *Test of Phonemic Awareness*, an informal assessment developed by Stahl and Murray, measures a child's ability to both segment and blend phonemes. It is an excellent screening tool to help assess emergent reading abilities.[2] This assessment is individually administered and contains two parts. For each part, the instructor reads the provided instructions to the child and writes down his or her responses in the appropriate spaces.

[1]*Onset* refers to any beginning consonant, and *rime* is the vowel and any final consonant. For example, in the word *stamp*, "st" is the onset and "amp" is the rime.

[2]The Test of Phonemic Awareness presented here has been shortened from its original version as advised by the author. (Private conversation, April, 1993.)

TEST OF PHONEMIC AWARENESS*

I. Blending

> *Instructions:* Say to the child: "I'm going to say some words in secret code, spreading out the sounds until they come out one at a time. Guess what word I'm saying. For example, if I say /h/-/a/-/m/, you say *ham*." Give feedback for practice words. Use additional examples if necessary. When the idea is clear, discontinue feedback. Say, "Now try these."

Examples and practice words

1. Segmented 3-phoneme words

f-un	fun	_____	m-a-p	map	_____
k-ing	king	_____	t-e-n	ten	_____
s-o-me	some	_____	s-e-t	set	_____
p-u-t	put	_____	d-i-d	did	_____
s-e-n-d	send	_____	sh-ee-p	sheep	_____

2. Blended onset

3. Blended rime

f-l-a-t	flat	_____	f-i-n-d	find	_____
c-r-a-ck	crack	_____	p-i-/ng/-k	pink	_____
s-p-a-ce	space	_____	c-a-m-p	camp	_____
p-l-ai-n	plain	_____	w-i-l-d	wild	_____
s-t-e-p	step	_____	l-a-s-t	last	_____

II. Phoneme Isolation

> *Instructions:* Say to the child: "This time I want you to listen for just one sound in a word. Tell me the sound you hear at the beginning of each word I say. For example, if I say *fix*, you say /f/." See Part I instructions for note on practice words.

Examples and practice words

no	/n/	_____	hot	/h/	_____
ship	/sh/	_____	jump	/j/	_____
time	/t/	_____			

*"Phonemic Segmentation Test" developed by Steven A. Stahl and Bruce A. Murray. Presented at American Research Association, April, 1993. Reprinted with permission of Steven A. Stahl and Bruce A. Murray.

Phoneme Isolation, continued

1. Onset-rime			2. Blended onset		
food	/f/	_____	flood	/f/	_____
came	/k/	_____	cross	/k/	_____
side	/s/	_____	speak	/s/	_____
pad	/p/	_____	please	/p/	_____
seal	/s/	_____	state	/s/	_____

Instructions: Say to the child: " Now I want you to listen and tell me the sound at the very end of each word I say. For example, if I say *watch*, you say /ch/." See Part I instructions for note on practice words.

Examples and practice words

off	/f/	_____	egg	/g/	_____
fish	/sh/	_____			

3. Rime V-C			4. Blended rime		
room	/m/	_____	sand	/d/	_____
not	/t/	_____	junk	/k/	_____
gas	/s/	_____	limp	/p/	_____
sled	/d/	_____	build	/d/	_____
cross	/s/	_____	best	/t/	_____

Scoring: Score one point for each correct response. Students scoring at least 50 percent correct in each section (eight items in Blending and ten items in Phoneme Isolation) are demonstrating levels of awareness that correspond to emergent reading and writing success.

ASSESSING SPELLING STAGES

Researchers have categorized several stages of spelling development. Those stages are linked to emergent reading and writing ability. The term **invented spelling** is used to describe these early stages of spelling development.

There are five stages of invented spelling. These stages have characteristics or features that will be easily recognizable after some practice with children's writing.

Characteristics of Prephonemic Spelling

The *prephonemic spelling* stage is typical of older preschoolers, kindergartners, and many first-graders. Its characteristics are as follows:

1. The word is made up of letters and letterlike forms, such as numerals and incorrectly formed or made-up letters.
2. The word is unreadable; letters and forms are used randomly and do not represent sounds.
3. The word is usually arranged in a horizontal line.
4. The story may be made up of unbroken lines of letters or arranged in wordlike configurations with spaces between them.
5. Writing shows that the child is aware that words are made up of letters and that print is arranged horizontally.

Characteristics of Early Phonemic Spelling

The *early phonemic spelling* stage is typical of very beginning readers, some kindergartners, most first-graders, and some older children just beginning to read.

1. The word is made up entirely of letters, usually in short strings of one to four letters; single letters are often used to represent whole words.
2. The word represents the discovery of the alphabetic principle: letters are used to represent some of the sounds in words.
3. Writing commonly features the use of consonants to represent initial sounds; sometimes final sounds and/or other important, clearly discernible sounds are represented too, but the spellings are very incomplete.
4. Writing shows the child's discovery that letters in print represent sound in spoken words and indicates the beginning of the ability to segment phonemes.

Characteristics of Letter-name Spelling

The *letter-name spelling* stage is typical of beginning readers who can read a little but are not yet fluent. Most first- and many second-graders fall into this group.

1. Writing shows the child's firm awareness that letters represent sounds, so the letters they use stand for sounds with no silent letters included.
2. The word is still incomplete. Some sounds clearly evident in words are systematically omitted, such as *m*'s and *n*'s before consonants, vowels in

unstressed syllables, and many short vowels until late in this stage. However, more sound features are represented than in earlier spelling stages.

3. The child uses the names of letters to represent sounds in words as well as the sounds of letters.

4. Spelling is often characterized by long vowels used appropriately, but unmarked (as with a silent *e*); short vowels predictably substituted by using vowel letter-names or omitted altogether; tense and plural endings spelled as the sound: *t*, *d*, and *id*; *s*, *z*, and *iz*; use of *jr*, *gr*, and *chr* for sounds adults spell with *er* and *dr*.

Characteristics of Transitional Spelling

The *transitional spelling* stage is typical of young pupils beyond the beginning reading stage and older ones who are still not fluent readers.

1. Spelling is nearly complete; all phonemes are represented, long and short vowel sounds are generally spelled correctly or typically: *hed* (head).

2. The child shows an awareness of marking systems, such as silent letters and consonant doubling, but uses markers inappropriately: *runing* (running), *makking* (making), *ducke* (duck).

3. The word is largely readable by others.

4. The writing may reveal several different attempts at the same word, sometimes abandoning a correct for an incorrect spelling.

5. Writing shows an awareness of inflectional endings, but the words are often spelled phonemically: *pickt* (picked) *wantid* (wanted).

Features List Analysis Forms* for Assessing Spelling Stages

Assessment of spelling stages can be done informally using a Features List (Gillet & Temple, 1990) or by examining the child's writing. By comparing the child's spelling attempts to the actual spelling of the word, teachers can determine the child's spelling stage. Examples of the two features lists are provided on the following pages.

Directions for Using the Features List

Select the appropriate features list for administration. The Beginners' Features List is suitable for grades K–2. The Advanced Features List is for students in grades 3 and up. Administer the list as a traditional spelling test.

1. Say the word in isolation.

2. Read the sentence using the word.

3. Repeat the word two or three times in isolation, if needed.

Children should be encouraged to attempt each word. Let them know you are not expecting correct spelling, just their best effort.

*From *Understanding Reading Problems: Assessment and Instruction* by Jean Wallace Gillet and Charles Temple. Copyright © 1990 by Jean Wallace Gillet and Charles Temple. Reprinted with permission of HarperCollins Publishers.

Beginners' Features List (Grades K–2)

1. late   Kathy was late to school today.
2. wind   The wind blew the door shut.
3. shed   A snake will shed its skin.
4. geese   Geese and ducks like to swim.
5. jumped   The frog jumped into the pond.
6. yell   Don't yell in the hall.
7. chirped   The baby birds chirped loudly.
8. once   Each person may vote once.
9. learned   Have you learned all the rules?
10. shove   Shove the desks out of the way.
11. trained   He trained his dog to sit up.
12. year   What grade were you in last year?
13. shock   She got a shock from that lamp.
14. stained   The ink stained my shirt.
15. chick   A baby chick hatched from the egg.
16. drive   My sister is learning to drive.

Advanced Features List (Grades 3 and up)

1. setter   Her dog is an Irish setter.
2. shove   Don't shove when you line up.
3. grocery   I'm going to the grocery store.
4. button   Did you lose a button from your shirt?
5. sailor   My cousin is a good sailor.
6. prison   The robber will go to prison.
7. nature   We walked on the nature trail.
8. peeked   He peeked at the answers to the test.
9. special   Tomorrow is a special day.
10. preacher   The preacher talked for over an hour.
11. slowed   We slowed down on the bumpy road.
12. sail   The boat had a torn sail.
13. feature   We saw a double feature at the movies.
14. batter   The first batter struck out.

FEATURES LIST ANALYSIS FORM (BEGINNER)

Student _____ Date _____

_____

Test Word	Student's Response	Classification	Score
1. late			
2. wind			
3. shed			
4. geese			
5. jumped			
6. yell			
7. chirped			
8. once			
9. learned			
10. shove			
11. trained			
12. year			
13. shock			
14. stained			
15. chick			
16. drive			

Total _____

Stage	Number of Responses
Prephonemic	_____
Early Phonemic	_____
Letter-name	_____
Transitional	_____
Correct	_____

Stage of Development _____

FEATURES LIST ANALYSIS FORM (ADVANCED)

Student _____ Date _____

_____

Test Word	Student's Response	Classification	Score
1. setter			
2. shove			
3. grocery			
4. button			
5. sailor			
6. prison			
7. nature			
8. peeked			
9. special			
10. preacher			
11. slowed			
12. sail			
13. feature			
14. batter			

Total _____

Stage	Number of Responses
Prephonemic	_____
Early Phonemic	_____
Letter-name	_____
Transitional	_____
Correct	_____

Stage of Development _____

USING THE FEATURES LIST ANALYSIS FORM

Directions: In this activity, you are given a list of test words with the child's written responses. Classify each response as one of the five spelling stages. Score each stage according to the following key, multiplying the amount of responses for each stage by the corresponding number:

1 = Prephonemic

2 = Early Phonemic

3 = Letter-name

4 = Transitional

5 = Correct

Determine the spelling stage by adding up the scores and dividing the total by the total number of words in the list. The resulting number (which corresponds to the above key) indicates the stage; thus, 2.8 would indicate a child was leaving the early phonemic stage and was very close to the letter-name stage.

Place the number of responses for each stage in the appropriate line on the Features List Analysis Form. The number of words at each stage help to determine if a student is solidly in a stage, just entering a stage, or close to leaving a stage. A large number of words in any one stage indicates the student is currently performing at that stage of spelling development. For example:

Stage	Key Number		Number of Responses		Score
Prephonemic	1	×	2	=	2
Early Phonemic	2	×	10	=	20
Letter-name	3	×	3	=	9
Transitional	4	×	1	=	4
Correct	5	×	0	=	0
				Total points	35

Total points ÷ Total words on list = 35 ÷ 16 = 2.1

Stage of Development: This student is clearly at an Early Phonemic stage of spelling development.

FEATURES LIST ANALYSIS FORM (BEGINNER)

Student ___Lauren_____ Date __9/17/93_____

Test Word	Student's Response	Classification	Score
1. late	lat		
2. wind	wnd		
3. shed	shed		
4. geese	gez		
5. jumped	jumpt		
6. yell	yell		
7. chirped	chipt		
8. once	wons		
9. learned	lerd		
10. shove	sov		
11. trained	chand		
12. year	yer		
13. shock	shock		
14. stained	stand		
15. chick	chick		
16. drive	driv		

Total _____

Stage	Number of Responses
Prephonemic	_____
Early Phonemic	_____
Letter-name	_____
Transitional	_____
Correct	_____

Stage of Development _____

FEATURES LIST ANALYSIS FORM (ADVANCED)

Student ___*Muhamed*___ Date ___*9/30/93*___

Test Word	Student's Response	Classification	Score
1. setter	str		
2. shove	shov		
3. grocery	gosere		
4. button	buton		
5. sailor	sellor		
6. prison	proson		
7. nature	nature		
8. peeked	peekt		
9. special	special		
10. preacher	precher		
11. slowed	slod		
12. sail	sell		
13. feature	fetre		
14. batter	bater		

Total _____

Stage	Number of Responses
Prephonemic	_____
Early Phonemic	_____
Letter-name	_____
Transitional	_____
Correct	_____

Stage of Development _____

| A C T I V I T Y |

USING CHILDREN'S WRITING TO DETERMINE SPELLING STAGE

Directions: Following are examples of two children's writings. For each child, determine the stage of spelling development. Utilize the same technique applied in the features list by comparing the child's written word with the real word and classifying each word into one of the spelling stages or as correctly spelled. Then, total the number of words in each spelling stage to determine the child's stage of spelling development. Use the Developmental Spelling Stage Form to assist you in this activity.

YOUCANusceLRinACALRBOC

Writing Sample 1

"You can use colors in a coloring book."

The White Cat

But I Wnot to cep him Nick
Said Butyou Can⁼t Said
father But Wit if it Be lang
to hes owners ast Tim

Sanowbillb

Writing Sample 2

The White Cat
But I want to keep him, Nick said. But you can't said father.
But what if it belongs to his owners? asked Tim.

DEVELOPMENTAL SPELLING STAGE FORM

Student _____ Date _____

Test Word/ Real Word	Student's Response	Classification	Score

Stage	Number of Responses
Prephonemic	_____
Early Phonemic	_____
Letter-name	_____
Transitional	_____
Correct	_____

Stage of Development _____

SUMMARY

It is often advisable to assess a student's sight word recognition and word-analysis skills. This chapter discussed ways to assess word analysis, phonemic segmentation, and sight word knowledge. In addition, the chapter offered practice in determining a child's developmental spelling level. The use of these assessments with other measures, such as the IRI and observation, help to complete the picture of a child's reading strengths and needs.

SUGGESTED READINGS

Gillet, J., & Temple, C. (1990). *Understanding reading problems* (3rd ed.). Glenview, IL: Scott, Foresman/Little, Brown.

Maggart, Z. R., & Zintz, M. V. (1990). *Corrective reading* (6th ed.). Dubuque, IA: Wm. C. Brown. Ch. 3.

Rubin, D. (1991). *Diagnosis and correction in reading instruction* (2nd ed.). Boston: Allyn & Bacon.

Wilson, R. M., & Cleland, C. J. (1989). *Diagnostic and remedial reading for classroom and clinic* (6th ed.). Columbus, OH: Merrill Publishing Company.

9/

GROUPING AND INSTRUCTIONAL DECISION MAKING

This chapter presents a number of activities that require synthesizing the information acquired from activities in Chapters 3–8. In each activity in this chapter, there are a variety of test data to examine in order to make both grouping and instructional decisions. In real life, decisions are based on more information than will be presented here. The intent of this chapter is to encourage evaluation and synthesis of data from different sources.

Teachers make decisions daily. Instructional decisions include the objectives to emphasize, the materials to be used, the instructional methods to employ, the pace of the instruction, and the classroom organization. Grouping decisions deal with group membership organization and grouping strategies.

GROUPING

One of the major decisions teachers face is how to organize for reading instruction. Most of us learned to read in classrooms using a three-group reading structure. Students of similar reading achievement in this organizational pattern were grouped together and met with the teacher for daily reading instruction.

The three groups probably used different materials or different-level texts. Or the groups may have used the same text but a different pace of instruction. Regrouping like students together in small groups increased student participation, provided for individualized instruction, and maximized the teacher's time. There is, however, criticism of total class homogeneous grouping. Current research on grouping indicates that homogeneous classes do not produce achievement gains over heterogeneous classes. However, regrouping students by achievement for mathematics and reading appears to increase student achievement in those subject areas. Thus, within-class grouping appears to be an acceptable grouping strategy (Slavin, 1987).

Whole-class instruction is appropriate under certain conditions. That is, in teaching vocabulary, oral language, listening, common learnings, or guided reading in which each child has a personal copy of the book, whole-class instruction then makes sense. However, there should be opportunities for children to meet in small groups to discuss the reading. Group cohesiveness is facilitated when membership is limited to two to six members. Groups larger than fifteen will not allow maximum participation for the members (Francis, 1988).

In addition to discussion, small groups are beneficial for direct instruction in specific skills and/or strategies needed by the children. Not all children will be in all specific skills or strategy teaching groups, and once the objective has been met, the group is disbanded.

Perhaps grouping has received a bad reputation because group membership was static. There were teachers who made grouping decisions at the beginning of the year and never changed the group membership even though the children changed. Group membership must be considered flexible, and as such, continuous assessment of students' progress is necessary.

Whether a teacher uses the basal method with the entire class placed in the same level or uses a literature-based model, we recommend that whole-class guided reading be supplemented with small-group guided reading and flexible membership reading groups for direct instruction of reading strategies and skills.

A C T I V I T Y

GROUPING FOR READING USING INFORMAL READING INVENTORY SCORES (GRADE 5)*

The purpose of this activity is to provide practice in grouping a class for reading instruction using IRI scores and determining the appropriate basal level for each group.

Directions: Read the following scenario, and from the IRI test results:

1. determine the students' reading levels
2. group the students into appropriate reading groups (no more than four groups)
3. determine a basal reader level (2-1, 2-2, 3-1, 3-2, etc.) for the group; assume that you have only one basal series available in the school, but you may use any book level that would be suitable to the groups' reading levels.

Hint: You will find that some of the students have a different word-recognition reading level from their comprehension reading level on a test passage. Your grouping will need to consider both the word-recognition and comprehension skills of the children.

---

*This activity is a revised version of an activity developed by William Powell (1976). Used with permission.

Scenario

You are a new fifth-grade teacher in a small school district. It is early September, and you were hired after the start of the school year because a teacher became ill.

You find that there is very little test information available on your students, but they have been placed into two reading groups. One group has twelve children reading in the fifth-grade basal (there's only one basal for the fifth grade). The second reading group has eight children in the 4-2 basal. These children attended summer school in order not to be retained in fourth grade.

After one week of working with the children, you feel that some of them have been incorrectly placed in the basal. You decide to administer an IRI to each child. On the following pages are the results of your testing and the basal level for each child before IRI administration.

Informal Reading Inventory Scores and Basal Reader Levels

Student	Passage Grade Level	Word-recognition Percent Correct	Comprehension Percent Correct	Basal Level
Andrea	3	97%	90%	5
	4	96%	89%	
	5	94%	85%	
	6	90%	60%	
Carrie	1	95%	90%	4-2
	2	96%	80%	
	3	95%	70%	
	4	95%	55%	
Darren	2	95%	75%	4-2
	3	85%	50%	
Evelyn	4	100%	85%	5
	5	98%	80%	
	6	95%	65%	
	7	95%	60%	
Gavin	3	95%	100%	5
	4	93%	90%	
	5	90%	85%	
Harriet	4	100%	95%	5
	5	98%	85%	
	6	95%	60%	
Harry	4	96%	70%	5
	5	94%	50%	
	6	90%	40%	

Student	Passage Grade Level	Word-recognition Percent Correct	Comprehension Percent Correct	Basal Level
Jennifer	5	100%	100%	5
	6	100%	95%	
	7	100%	90%	
Kedrick	2	95%	80%	5
	3	95%	80%	
	4	94%	50%	
	5	90%	40%	
Mary	3	97%	90%	5
	4	94%	60%	
	5	94%	50%	
	6	90%	40%	
Monte	2	90%	70%	4-2
	3	90%	50%	
Nadine	3	98%	80%	4-2
	4	95%	70%	
	5	93%	50%	
Peter	3	100%	80%	5
	4	95%	80%	
	5	92%	70%	
	6	94%	60%	
Ron	1	100%	75%	4-2
	2	98%	70%	
	3	94%	50%	
	4	92%	50%	

Student	Passage Grade Level	Word-recognition Percent Correct	Comprehension Percent Correct	Basal Level
Sabrina	4	95%	100%	5
	5	95%	90%	
	6	94%	80%	
	7	90%	70%	
Terry	3	98%	90%	5
	4	95%	80%	
	5	85%	70%	
Wesley	1	95%	80%	4-2
	2	90%	70%	
	3	85%	50%	
Wilma	4	100%	100%	5
	5	100%	100%	
	6	98%	90%	
	7	95%	80%	
Yvonne	3	95%	50%	4-2
	4	92%	30%	
Zenia	2	100%	90%	4-2
	3	95%	50%	
	4	90%	40%	

Questions

1. As you were forming your reading groups, what posed the most problem for you?

2. On what basis did you group students?

3. Which students do you feel were placed inappropriately in the original grouping? Why?

4. What additional information would you like to have, and for which children?

ACTIVITY

GROUPING FOR READING USING STANDARDIZED TEST SCORES (GRADE 5)

Directions: You are a fifth-grade teacher. The students in your class range in ability and achievement level. The test data provided are based on an achievement test given in the spring of fourth grade. Using the information on the following pages:

1. group the students into tentative reading groups
2. identify students with a possible reading problem
3. describe the reading approach(es) you would use with your class

Standardized Test Scores in Reading Vocabulary, Comprehension, and Listening

Student	Reading Vocabulary		Reading Comprehension		Listening	
	NP*	GE*	NP*	GE*	NP*	GE*
Nicholas	18	2.9	1	1.9	39	4.1
Nicole	46	4.5	76	7.3	39	4.1
Deidre	57	5.2	68	6.1	24	3.5
Manuel	13	2.8	9	2.5	34	3.9
Joel	9	2.6	3	2.2	13	2.9
Tony	70	5.8	28	3.3	62	5.4
Cathy	49	4.7	65	5.7	29	3.7
Nadia	45	4.5	44	4.5	17	3.1
Antonia	23	3.2	1	1.9	4	2.0
Erica	11	2.7	28	3.3	13	2.9
Alex	4	2.3	2	2.0	6	2.4
Brad	9	2.6	5	2.3	44	4.5
Adam	35	3.8	13	2.6	20	3.3
Matthew	9	2.6	22	3.0	6	2.4
Michelle	70	5.8	83	8.4	77	6.7
Joseph	10	2.7	11	2.6	6	2.4
Brandie	18	2.9	28	3.3	29	3.7
Christy	26	3.3	16	2.7	20	3.3

*NP = National Percentile.

GE = Grade Equivalent.

INSTRUCTIONAL DECISION MAKING

Another source of information that teachers can use to make decisions is standardized diagnostic test scores. A standardized diagnostic test will often provide a more in-depth look at a student's performance in a specific area, such as reading, than a general achievement test, which gives a global view of the student's performance. Thus, a diagnostic test provides information on the student's vocabulary and comprehension skills, including phonics, structural analysis, literal comprehension, inferential comprehension, etc.

Diagnostic tests are often criterion-referenced; that is, they allow the teacher to judge the student's performance against a standard. A teacher can group students who have not met the established criterion in a particular area for skill/strategy instruction in that area.

While standardized diagnostic tests are a valuable source of information, they are not traditionally administered in large-scale, district-wide assessments. The responsibility for administration and scoring fall upon the classroom teacher or reading specialist in the school.

A C T I V I T Y

DECISION MAKING BASED ON STANDARDIZED TEST DATA (GRADE 4 SPECIAL READING CLASS)

Directions: On the following pages, you will find standardized test data for a fourth-grade reading class. The fifteen students were placed into the special reading class for the entire year based on their scores on other standardized tests given in April of their third-grade year.

The data are organized in two charts. The first gives raw scores and corresponding stanines for each student in vocabulary and comprehension. The second provides data for specific reading skill areas, derived from an **item analysis**. The subtest on structural analysis is broken down into word division (syllabication) and word blending. The scores presented for structural analysis are raw scores, but a criterion index (an indicator of average performance) is provided below the column label to evaluate each student's performance. The criterion index for structural analysis is 30 for third grade. Thus, a student who scored 15 correct on the blending subtest would be considered below average in this area compared to the norm for students in the third grade.

The comprehension subtest is broken down into literal and inferential scores. These scores are reported in stanines.

Examine the data given on the charts and then answer the questions that follow.

Standardized Diagnostic Reading Test Scores:
Vocabulary and Comprehension

Student	Auditory Vocabulary Raw Score	Stanine	Total Comprehension Raw Score	Stanine
Alex	32	6	41	4
Keona	28	5	35	3
George	26	5	21	2
Cecil	18	3	29	3
Rodney	37	7	29	3
Jerry	24	4	37	3
Will	18	3	24	2
Bryan	12	2	31	3
Mark	11	1	26	2
Isaac	7	1	26	2
Kris	17	3	24	2
Melissa	22	4	28	3
Joyce	18	3	21	2
Pat	6	1	15	1
Angela	19	3	33	3

Standardized Diagnostic Reading Test Scores:
Item Analysis

Student	Structural Analysis Raw Score		Comprehension Stanine	
	Word Division CI = 30*	Blending CI = 30*	Literal	Inferential
Alex	21	17	4	4
Keona	24	14	3	3
George	13	13	2	2
Cecil	9	18	3	3
Rodney	24	19	2	3
Jerry	24	20	3	3
Will	19	19	2	2
Bryan	12	5	3	3
Mark	17	21	1	1
Isaac	25	17	2	3
Kris	15	9	2	3
Melissa	25	17	2	3
Joyce	11	13	1	2
Pat	15	17	1	1
Angela	22	13	3	3

*Refer to page 228 for an explanation of CI (Criterion Index).

Questions

1. Group the students based on their reading level. Keep to a maximum of four groups.

    Group 1   Group 2   Group 3   Group 4

2. Group students for specific skill instruction, and indicate what skill instruction they should receive.

3. Design a lesson for one of these specific skill groups.

4. Design a direct-instruction lesson for the whole class in an area of need.

5. Based on the standardized test data provided, give at least four observations you can make about this class.

6. Describe the type of reading approach you would use, and tell why you think it would be appropriate.

EXAMINING A READING GROUP'S PERFORMANCE
(GRADE 2)

Directions: Read the following scenario, review the data presented, and answer the questions that follow. Use the Powell criteria (see Chapter 6) to interpret the IRI scores.

It is November, and your reading groups are established. The students were placed into their prospective groups based on the end-of-year standardized test scores and teacher recommendation. While some students are handling the basal text with ease, others do not seem to be progressing at all. In particular, one reading group seems to present you the greatest challenge, and you question the appropriateness of the placement of the students.

You have gathered the test data available on that reading group. These test data include the standardized test scores from an achievement test given in early September and results of an IRI that you administered in late September. You have also conducted a structured observation of the group's word-recognition abilities during an oral reading session. The results from these three diagnostic measures are given on the following pages.

Achievement Tests: Primary

Stanine Scores

Student	Reading Comprehension Stanine	Sight Vocabulary Stanine	Phoneme-Grapheme Consonants Stanine	Vocabulary in Context Stanine	Word Part Clues Stanine
Sherman	4	4	5	4	3
Brenda	3	4	4	3	4
Emma	5	4	6	5	5
Brad	5	6	6	4	3
Wes	3	4	6	3	3
Lucinda	4	4	4	3	3

Informal Reading Inventory

Student	Passage Grade Level	Word-recognition Percent Correct	Comprehension Percent Correct	Basal Level
Sherman	1 2	90% 90%	70% 60%	2-1
Brenda	1 2	88% 90%	65% 50%	2-1
Emma	1 2	93% 90%	100% 90%	2-1
Brad	1 2	95% 100%	90% 75%	2-1
Wes	1 2	85% 80%	60% 50%	2-1
Lucinda	1 2	93% 88%	70% 65%	2-1

Observation Record: Word-identification Skills

	Sherman	Brenda	Emma	Brad	Wes	Lucinda
1. Pronounces basic sight words in isolation.	S	S	A	A	S	S
2. Pronounces basic sight words in context.	S	S	A	A	S	S
3. Uses phonic principles in decoding unknown words.	A	S	A	S	N	S
4. Pronounces morphemic units in words.	S	S	S	S	N	N
5. Decodes words using syllabic units, rather than individual letter sounds.	S	S	S	S	N	N
6. Uses context to read unfamiliar words.	S	N	S	S	N	N

Key:
A = Always
S = Sometimes
N = Never

Questions

1. Is Wes properly placed in a reading group? Why, or why not?

2. Wes is, obviously, having reading problems. What are his reading difficulties? What evidence led you to this conclusion?

3. What observations have you made about the other members of the group?

4. Before making a referral, the classroom teacher should institute an instructional change. What would you do, and why?

5. What additional diagnostic information would you like to have, and for which children? Why?

6. Suppose that Wes's IQ is estimated at 105. His chronological age is 7 years 5 months. Does he have a reading disability? Why do you say that?

7. Plan a lesson in an area of need for the group.

8. Plan a lesson for Wes.

SUMMARY

This chapter offered practice in making decisions based on a variety of data sources. In the real classroom, you will make decisions based on more information than was given here; with the continuous assessment process, you will make informed, sound decisions regarding instruction, grouping practices, and material selection.

SUGGESTED READINGS

Cheek, E. H., Flippo, R., & Lindsey, J. (1989). *Reading for success in elementary schools*. Chicago: Holt, Rinehart & Winston. Ch. 13.

Duffy, G., & Roehler, L. R. (1989). *Improving classroom reading instruction: A decision making approach* (2nd ed.). New York: Random House.

Mason, J. M., & Au, K. H. (1990). *Reading instruction for today* (2nd ed.). Glenview, IL: Scott, Foresman/Little, Brown.

Vacca, J. L., Vacca, R. T., & Gove, M. K. (1991). *Reading and learning to read* (2nd ed.) New York: HarperCollins Publishers.

APPENDIX A

DIRECTIONS FOR THE DIRECTED LISTENING-THINKING ACTIVITY

The directed listening-thinking activity (DLTA) can be used as an informal assessment activity for prereading skills. Developed by Stauffer (1980), it is actually a teaching activity for predicting, summarizing, and evaluating. Combined with oral retelling of the story, the technique can provide valuable insights into the child's stage of emergent literacy.

The DLTA is conducted with a storybook or picture book with a strong plot. If the story is to be used with a small group, the book should be large enough for all to see the pictures.

PHASE I

The teacher begins the DLTA by showing the students the cover and reading the title. The teacher then encourages thinking by asking: "What do you think this is going to be about? What makes you think that?" (With content material, one might ask: "What words do you think will be in the passage? What do you think this passage is about?") All students' responses are accepted and written on the board.

PHASE II

The teacher reads a portion of the selection aloud. At each stopping point, the teacher asks: "What has happened so far? Which of our predictions were correct? Why? Can we eliminate any predictions? What do you think might happen next?"

The reading continues with the predicting-listening-proving cycle. It seems best to keep the number of stops to a maximum of four. More than four stopping points interrupts the flow of the story, and children could lose story continuity. With long stories, the teacher may use the DLTA with the first half of the story and then read the second half without interruption.

PHASE III

Once the story is completed, the teacher can ask students to retell the story in their own words. In this phase, the teacher observes oral language skills, awareness of story structure, sequencing skills, and short-term memory.

APPENDIX B/

DIRECTIONS FOR THE LANGUAGE EXPERIENCE APPROACH

The language experience approach (LEA) is an instructional reading method, but the dictated story and rereadings can have value as an informal diagnostic technique with a small group or an individual child. The core of the approach is the development of children-dictated stories that are the product of experiences or are a natural result of spontaneous events that occur in the classroom.

To conduct a language experience lesson, the teacher needs the following:

1. a stimulus, such as a concrete object or actual experience (trip, holiday, etc.)
2. a pad of large newsprint
3. a felt pen or crayon

The lesson begins with the concrete stimulus. The children discuss the stimulus orally, usually with leading questions by the teacher. All children who want to express themselves should have an opportunity to do so. This stage is very important in gathering data on a child's oral language skills and preparing the children for the dictation phase.

After the experience (or object) has been discussed, the teacher explains to the children that they are going to write a story about the experience (or object) and that everyone will contribute a sentence.

Each child then provides a sentence. The teacher writes down *exactly* what the child says and reads each word clearly as it is printed on the pad.

When the story is completed, the teacher reads the entire story two or three times, using a left-to-right hand motion to guide the reading. The teacher should use natural phrasing and provide a good model of oral reading.

Then the children read the story aloud with the teacher. Individual volunteers may read a sentence or, if possible, the whole story.

Dictated stories can be used on successive days for illustration, rereading, learning sight words, or working on some prereading and/or reading skill.

Upon completion of a language experience lesson, teachers should ask themselves the following questions to encourage reflection on the language experience event.

1. Was the topic of the story a shared experience? Did all the children participate in the experience?
2. Was there enough time allowed for discussion?
3. Did all the children in the group participate in the discussion?
4. Was each sentence repeated by the teacher as it was written?
5. Was a left-to-right direction smoothly emphasized by the teacher when the story was read aloud?
6. Was the story read with rhythm and expression?
7. Was the story read by the group at least three times?
8. Was the story accessible to those children who wanted to read it again?

APPENDIX C/

EXTRA FORMS

The following pages contain a blank Oral Reading Behavior Analysis Form, Summary Sheet, and a Cloze Test Applied Error Analysis Sheet for your use.

ORAL READING BEHAVIOR ANALYSIS FORM

Student _____ Date of Testing _____

Passage Grade Level _____

Text Word	Student's Response	Semantic Appropriateness	Syntactic Appropriateness	Graphic Similarity	Comments

(continue on back if needed)   Reading Level:_____ Ind. _____ Inst. _____Frus.

Word Accuracy Rate (number words correct/total words in passage) =

Self-correction (SC) Rate (number self-corrections/total errors) =

Words Aided or Prompted (words given by examiner):

Comprehension Accuracy Rate (number correct/total questions) =

Solving Strategies Used (See Questions to Determine Solving Strategies):

SUMMARY SHEET

Student _____ Grade _____ Sex _____

Birthdate _____ Chronological Age _____

School _____ Teacher _____

Test Administered by _____ Date of Testing _____

Independent Reading Level   _____

Instructional Reading Level   _____

Frustration Reading Level   _____

Listening Level   _____

Reading Strengths

Reading Needs

Instructional Recommendations

CLOZE TEST APPLIED ERROR
ANALYSIS SHEET

Student _____

Passage Grade Level _____

Material from Which Passage Was Derived _____

Date Administered _____

1. Exact Replacements _____

    Percent Correct _____

    Reading Level: _____ Independent _____ Instructional _____ Frustration

2. Total Errors _____

3. Determine the percent for each category of error.

Category	Number of Errors	Percent
SYN	_____	_____
SEM	_____	_____
SEM/NStc	_____	_____
STC	_____	_____
NON	_____	_____
OM	_____	_____

Possible Strategies Used

Needs

GLOSSARY

Advanced organizer   A method for preparing students to read by providing prereading activities or information.

Anecdotal records   An informal observation tool where observed behaviors are described.

Assessment   The ongoing gathering of information about students.

Auditory discrimination   The ability to hear differences in sounds.

Auditory perception   The capacity for obtaining information from sounds.

Basal reading method   A series of graded texts for reading instruction.

Big books   Large books used to familiarize children with print concepts and to provide positive book experiences.

Bottom-up model   A model of the reading process holding that readers acquire the ability to read by learning a hierarchy of skills.

Cloze test   An informal technique for instruction or assessment in which students fill in omitted words from a passage.

Cognitive confusion   A child's confusion concerning print concepts.

Cognitive processes   The processes of perceiving and knowing.

Comprehension   The process of constructing meaning.

Confidence level   Limits in a sample distribution between which a test score is expected to lie.

Context   The use of words surrounding an unknown word to determine the unknown word's meaning.

Corrective readers   Readers who have minor deficiencies in one or more skill areas.

Creative comprehension   Imaginative response to prose.

Critical comprehension   The level of comprehension where students can make evaluations and judgments.

Decoding   Analyzing words by identifying sound units.

Derived score   A unit into which a raw score is changed to facilitate its use for statistical analysis.

Developmental readers   Readers who are progressing normally for their age/grade.

Diagnosis Extensive examination through testing and observation of a student's strengths and weaknesses.

Direct instruction A strategy of teaching involving modeling, guided practice, and independent practice.

Directed listening-thinking activity (DLTA) An instructional and assessment strategy using listening, predicting, and confirming.

Directed reading activity (DRA) A technique for teaching reading, using preteaching strategies, silent reading, comprehension checks, oral rereading, and follow-up activities.

Directionality The left-to-right reading process, including the return sweep.

Emergent literacy The development of the ability to read; includes oral language development, understanding of print concepts, and development of phonemic awareness.

Formal tests Assessments with very specific directions and conditions for testing, typically standardized tests.

Frustration level The level at which the reader has difficulty with word recognition and comprehends with less than 70 percent accuracy.

Grade equivalent A derived score expressed in grade years and months.

Graphic similarity The similarity of letters between a text word and how a student says the word.

Imaging Creating mental pictures to help comprehension and word recognition.

Independent level The level at which the student can read and comprehend without teacher assistance.

Inferential comprehension The level of comprehension where the reader can make interpretations about text and find relationships among words to make meaning.

Informal reading inventory (IRI) An informal assessment instrument in which a child reads from graded passages and answers comprehension questions to determine independent, instructional, and frustration reading levels.

Informal tests Assessment instruments closely resembling classroom tasks, developed and administered by the classroom teacher.

Instructional level The reading level at which the student is challenged but not frustrated; some teacher assistance is needed.

Interactive reader A reader who uses strategies and skills while interacting with print.

Invented spelling Spelling words the way the child thinks they sound.

Item analysis An examination of individual items on a test in relation to the whole set of items.

Language experience approach (LEA) An integrative reading and writing approach using the student's experiences and words.

Linguistic strategies Strategies based on the use of word families and spelling patterns.

Listening age A measure of a child's listening achievement derived by adding 5.2 to a grade equivalent score obtained from a listening achievement measure.

Listening comprehension The highest grade-level material at which the student can comprehend what is being read to him or her with 70 percent or better accuracy.

Literal comprehension The level of comprehension where the reader can recall information.

Metacognitive skills The learner's ability to know how to learn, how to monitor his or her own learning, and how to evaluate his or her own learning.

Miscues Oral reading responses that are different from the written text.

Morphemic units The smallest meaning units of language: roots, prefixes, and suffixes.

Narrative story A story form in which a sequence of events is recounted.

Norm-referenced tests Standardized assessments intended to compare a student's performance with the performances of others.

Percentile rank A person's relative position within a defined group.

Perceptual processes Processes related to obtaining information from sensory stimulation.

Phonemic awareness The ability to hear and separate different sounds in words.

Phonic principles Rules of letter-sound correspondence that assist students in decoding words.

Portfolio A file of evidence to show student progress over time.

Potential reading level Possible, as opposed to actual, reading level. Often determined by listening comprehension assessment.

Prediction guide An informal assessment strategy that determines whether a student uses background knowledge in making predictions.

Prereading skills A term used before the recognition of emergent literacy to refer to the skills needed for beginning reading instruction.

Qualitative analysis Evaluation of the qualities or characteristics of miscues.

Quantitative analysis Evaluation of data that can be measured and described numerically to determine reading level.

Raw score The actual number of items correctly answered on a test.

Reading age A measure of a child's reading achievement derived by adding 5.2 to a grade equivalent score obtained from a reading achievement measure.

Reading expectancy The grade level at which the student is expected to be reading based on mental age or IQ.

Reading expectancy age Relates a child's mental age to his or her chronological age.

Reading expectancy quotient Relates a student's actual performance test score to the expected reading test score considering the student's mental age or IQ score.

Reading quotient Relates a child's reading age to his or her chronological age.

Reading readiness A term used to refer to a child's preparation for beginning reading instruction.

Reciprocal teaching A strategy designed to develop comprehension where students and teachers exchange roles in developing metacognitive strategies.

Remedial readers Readers who have severe problems and perform considerably below their potential level.

ReQuest procedure A comprehension strategy where students develop questions about a reading.

Running record An informal assessment of oral reading behaviors similar to miscue analysis.

Schema A building block of cognition in the mind.

Self-corrections Errors in oral reading that the student corrects on his or her own.

Semantic cues   Meaning-based aids for understanding a word or phrase.

Sight words   Common words students should recognize instantly, without analysis.

Speech-to-print match   The relationship of one printed word for every spoken word.

SQ3R   A study strategy — Survey, Question, Read, Recite, Review.

Standard error of measurement (SEM)   A statistical estimate of the error contained in a norm-referenced test.

Standard score   A derived score used for ease of test interpretation.

Standardized tests   Formal assessments administered under prescribed conditions.

Stanine   A normalized standard score of nine units, 1–9.

Story elements   The parts of a narrative (e.g., setting, characters, etc.).

Story frames   A form of a story map used for narratives using a series of spaces hooked together by transition words.

Story grammar   A form of a story map used for narratives.

Story map   A visual representation of the key elements of a narrative.

Story retelling   An instructional and assessment technique for comprehension in which a reader or listener tells what he or she remembers about a narrative.

Structural analysis   The strategy of using morphemes to identify words and determine their meanings.

Structured observation   Systematic observations of children's reading situations.

Syllabic units   Phonological segments of speech with a vowel or vowel-like sound.

Syntactic cues   Aids for understanding a word based on parts of speech and grammar.

Text structures   The organization of text (e.g., narrative and expository).

Top-down model   A model of the reading process that emphasizes the interactive process between the reader and the printed page.

Visual motor skills   Abilities requiring visual motor coordination.

REFERENCES

Alexander, J. E. (Ed.). (1988). *Teaching reading* (3rd ed.). Boston: Scott, Foresman.

Betts, E. (1946). *Foundation of reading instruction*. New York: American Book Company.

Clark, D. J., Clark, D. M., & Lovett, C. J. (1990). Changes in mathematics teaching call for assessment alternatives. In *1990 National Council of Teachers of Mathematics yearbook* (pp. 118–129). Reston, VA: National Council of Teachers of Mathematics.

Clay, M. M. (1985). *The early detection of reading difficulties* (3rd ed.). Auckland, New Zealand: Heinemann Publishers.

Clay, M. M. (1991). *Reading: Becoming literate* (3rd ed.). Auckland, New Zealand: Heinemann Publishers.

Downing, J. (1979). *Reading and reasoning*. New York: Springer-Verlag.

Francis, E. (1988). Group process. In J. T. Dillon (Ed.), *Questioning and discussion: A multidisciplinary study* (pp. 259–279). New Jersey: Ablex Publishing Company.

Gillet, J. W., & Temple, C. (1990). *Understanding reading problems* (3rd ed.). Glenview, IL: Scott, Foresman/Little, Brown.

Harris, T. L., & Hodges, R. E. (1981). *A dictionary of reading and related terms*. Newark: International Reading Association.

Harris, A. J., & Sipay, E. R. (1990). *How to increase reading ability: A guide to developmental and remedial methods* (9th ed.). New York: Longman.

Klesius, J., & Homan, S. (1980). *Klesius-Homan Phonics Test*. Unpublished manuscript, University of South Florida, Tampa.

Klesius, J., & Searls, E. (1985). *Modified concepts about print test*. Unpublished manuscript, University of South Florida, Tampa.

Manzo, A. V. (1970). Reading and questioning: The ReQuest procedure. *Reading Improvement, 7,* 80–83.

McGinnis, D. J., & Smith, D. E. (1982). *Analyzing and treating reading problems*. New York: Macmillan Publishing Company.

McWilliams, L., & Rakes, T. A. (1979). *Content inventories: English, social studies, science*. Dubuque, IA: Kendall/Hunt Publishing Company.

Morrow, L. M. (1988). Retelling stories as a diagnostic tool. In S. M. Glazer, L. W. Searfoss, & L. M. Gentile (Eds.), *Re-examining reading diagnosis: New trends and procedures.* Newark: International Reading Association.

Palinscar, A. S., & Brown, A. L. (1985). Reciprocal teaching: Activities to promote "reading in your mind." In T. L. Harris & E. J. Cooper (Eds.), *Reading, thinking, and concept development* (pp. 147–159). New York: College Entrance Examination Board.

Powell, W. (1971). Validity of the I. R. I. reading levels. *Elementary English, 48,* 637–642.

Raker, T. A., & Smith, L. (1986). Assessing reading skills in the content areas. In E. K. Dishner, T. W. Bean, J. E. Readence, & D. W. Moore (Eds.), *Reading in the content areas: Improving classroom instruction* (2nd ed.). Dubuque, IA: Kendall/Hunt Publishing Company.

Rankin, E. F., & Culhane, J. W. (1969). Comparable cloze and multiple-choice comprehension test scores. *Journal of Reading, 13,* 193–198.

Readence, J. E., Bean, T. W., & Baldwin, R. S. (1989). *Content area reading: An integrated approach.* Dubuque, IA: Kendall/Hunt Publishing Company.

Richert, A. E. (1988). Teaching teachers to reflect: A consideration of program structure. In R. Barr, M. Kamil, P. Mosenthal, & P. D. Pearson (Eds.), *Handbook of reading research: Vol. 2.* New York: Longman.

Searfoss, L. W., & Readence, J. E. (1989). *Helping children learn to read.* Englewood Cliffs, NJ: Prentice Hall.

Shearer, A. P. (1982). A psycholinguistic comparison of second grade good readers and fourth grade good and poor readers on their oral reading miscues and standard and phoneme cloze responses. Doctoral dissertation, University of South Florida.

Slavin, R. E. (1987). Ability grouping and student achievement in elementary schools: A best evidence synthesis. *Review of Educational Research 57,* (3), 293–336.

Stahl, S. A., & Murray, B. A. (1993). Test of phonemic awareness. Presented at the American Educational Research Association, Atlanta, GA, April, 1993.

Stauffer, R. (1980). *The language experience approach to the teaching of reading* (2nd ed.). New York: Harper & Row.

Vacca, J. L., Vacca, R. T., & Gove, M. K. (1991). *Reading and learning to read* (2nd ed.). New York: HarperCollins.

Wilson, R. M., & Cleland, C. J. (1985). *Diagnostic and remedial reading for classroom and clinic* (5th ed.). Columbus, OH: Merrill Publishing Company.

INDEX